the EDIBLE ASIAN GARDEN

Rosalind Creasy

PERIPLUS

First published in 2000 by
PERIPLUS EDITIONS (HK) LTD.,
with editorial offices at 153 Milk Street,
Boston, Massachusetts 02109 and
5 Little Road #08-01
Singapore 536983.

Library of Congress Cataloging-in-Publication Data is available.

ISBN: 962-593-300-X

Distributed by

USA
Tuttle Publishing
Distribution Center
364 Airport Industrial Park
North Clarendon,
VT 05759-9436
Tel: (802) 773-8930
Tel: (800) 526-2778

CANADA
Raincoast Books
8680 Cambie Street
Vancouver, Canada V6P 6M9
Tel: (604) 323-7100
Fax: (604) 323-2600

SOUTHEAST ASIA
Berkeley Books Pte. Ltd.
5 Little Road #08-01
Singapore 536983
Tel: (65) 280-3320
Fax: (65) 280-6290

JAPAN
Tuttle Shuppan
RK Building, 2nd floor
2-13-10 Shimo-Meguro,
Meguro-Ku
Tokyo 153-0064
Tel: (03) 5437-0171
Fax: (03) 5437-0755

First edition
05 04 03 02 01 00
10 9 8 7 6 5 4 3 2 1

Design by Kathryn Sky-Peck

PRINTED IN SINGAPORE

contents

the edible asian garden

Over twenty years ago, in preparing for a trip to Hong Kong, I wanted to become proficient at eating with chopsticks so as not to embarrass myself. I practiced by using them to pick up dry macaroni until I thought I had acquired some skill. For our first dinner in Hong Kong, my husband and I arrived at the restaurant starving. To begin the meal, the waiter placed a bowl of shiny, round Spanish peanuts in the middle of the table. Ah, food! I glanced around and discovered that the other diners were eating these nuts with their smooth, tapered chopsticks. Gamely, I plunged in—and onto the table went my peanut. Discreetly, I tried again and again in vain. Finally, I snared a nut—but squeezed too hard and, just as the waiter looked our way,

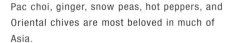

"sponged" it against the wall! So much for saving face!

Chopsticks aside, we had a wonderful time eating our way through Hong Kong. We dined on familiar stir-fries made with baby corn and pac choi, eggplants with garlic sauce, and asparagus with shrimp. But we also tried the unfamiliar—eels, sea cucumbers, and all sorts of vegetables, mushrooms, and ingredients we couldn't identify. Regardless of what dish we ordered, the seafood and vegetables were always fresh and the preparation

impeccable, and we thought the food, with few exceptions, the best we had ever eaten in our lives. I decided that if I were shipwrecked on an island and could have only one type of food for the rest of my life, this is what it would be—not my own native fare, not even French cuisine, but the food of the island of Hong Kong.

In fact, although we shopped, visited museums, and wandered around the waterfront, food in all its forms became our main interest in Hong Kong. We spent hours selecting restaurants from among the Japanese, Korean, and Chinese choices, and more hours choosing our food. We made numerous visits to the old part of the city, where herb stores abound and produce markets line the sidewalk. There we saw people walking down the street carrying water-filled plastic bags containing swimming fish, and string bags bulging with fresh bamboo shoots and unusual mushrooms. And

Pac choi, ginger, snow peas, hot peppers, and Oriental chives are most beloved in much of Asia.

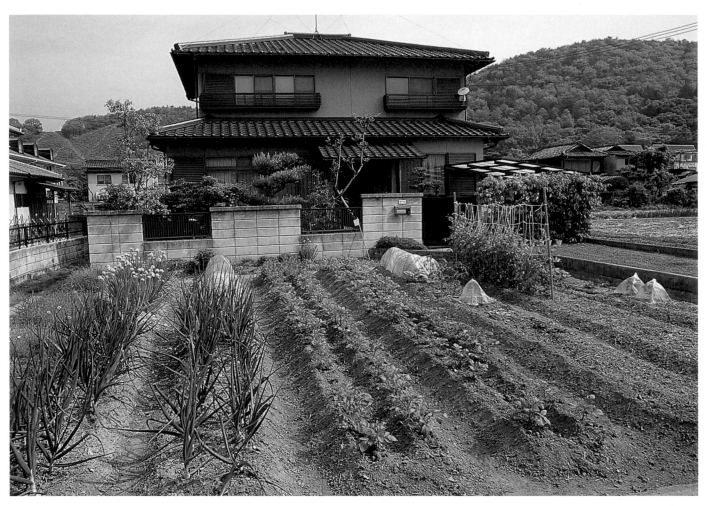

we saw all sorts of fresh greens—I couldn't get over the variety. Everywhere I looked were green, leafy vegetables I'd never seen before. Much to the shopkeepers' amusement (probably because we looked so puzzled as we hovered over the bins), we'd buy all sorts of unfamiliar fruits and vegetables and bring them back to our hotel to taste and photograph them. After laying out a towel to provide a neutral background, I'd set down a spoon to give the picture scale, lay out the edibles, and then photograph them one by one. Then, with the produce well documented, we'd taste everything and make notes.

That long-ago trip to Hong Kong opened my eyes to a whole new world of vegetables and cooking. It became obvious to me that the main focus of Chinese cuisine was on vegetables and that the varieties far exceeded my limited experience. It also became clear that the Chinese food I had eaten in restaurants at home only hinted at the heart of that cuisine. Because fresh Asian vegetables are the cornerstone of Chinese cooking, because restaurants in the United States generally can't obtain them, and, further, because the American audience is fixated on meat, what I had come across in the States was only a limited sample of Chinese cooking as a whole.

Once home, I began to research Asian cooking in earnest. I visited the community gardens of nearby

A typical vegetable garden in Japan is planted with onions, chives, and many different greens. As in much of Asia, the beds are in straight rows and raised above grade.

Southeast Asian neighborhoods and began to frequent Japanese and Thai restaurants to learn about tempura and curries. I sought out Chinese restaurants that prepared pea shoots and gai lon and a Japanese market that featured a whole section of Asian pickles with a tasting bar. As the years went by, accumulating information became much easier as northern California evolved into America's newest cultural melting pot, one brimming with folks from the Pacific Rim. Now I had Asian neighbors to share food and garden information with, huge new local grocery stores catering to a Japanese and Chinese clientele, and neighborhood markets devoted to East Indians and Southeast Asians—and mine to explore.

By now I've not only identified all the produce I collected in Hong Kong, I've grown and cooked with nearly all of the vegetables and herbs Asia has to offer. But I am but one gardener-cook, and Asian vegetables and food is a vast subject. I needed many other views. Fortunately, I have been able to spend hours with Asian chefs, including Ken Hom and Barbara Tropp, tour seed company trial plots, and work all over North America with home gardeners and cooks interested in Asian vegetables. One gardener in particular, David Cunningham, who was staff horticulturist at the Vermont Bean Seed Company, even grew an Asian demonstration garden for me to share with you.

Throughout this book, I give information on the vegetables and herbs of Japan, India, Korea, Southeast Asia, and the Philippines. You will soon see, however, that I have concentrated on the vegetables and cooking methods of the Chinese, as they cook with the greatest variety of vegetables and the seeds of their plants are the easiest of all Asian varieties for gardeners to obtain. Further, of all Oriental cooking styles, that of the Chinese is most accessible to Western cooks and uses the fewest unfamiliar techniques.

Before you lies a whole new range of vegetables and herbs: Shanghai flat cabbages, Chinese chives, Japanese mitsuba, and Thai basil. As a gardener and cook, you might well be embarking on a lifetime of exploration, and it's none too soon to start!

Farmer's markets around the country are often great places to purchase and learn more about Asian vegetables. Here at the Mt. View, California farmer's market are displays of bitter melon vines, water spinach, pac chois, long beans, and Asian eggplants.

how to grow an asian garden

Peter Chan's garden *(opposite)* is filled with Asian vegetables like pac choi and Asian squash, which in this case, because of cool Oregon summers, was planted in a tall planter box for extra warmth.

Many of the vegetables and herbs used in Asia are familiar to Westerners. In fact, we enjoy many cucumbers and winter squash varieties without even being aware that they come from Japanese breeding programs. Many of the so-called English cucumbers are examples. When you peruse seed catalogs looking for varieties, keep an eye out for sweet, "burpless" cucumbers such as 'Suyo Long' and 'Orient Express' and for dense, flavorful, nonstringy, sweet winter squash varieties such as 'Sweet Dumpling,' 'Red Kuri,' and 'Green Hokkaido.' Asian gardeners also breed and grow such familiar vegetables as eggplants, carrots, and turnips. Basic information on some of these vegetables is given in "The Encyclopedia of Asian Vegetables." Still, many Asian vegetables and herbs are unfamiliar to Western cooks and gardeners and it is on these that I concentrate most of my attention.

In much of Asia, land for cultivation is scarce and highly revered. Unlike many Western gardeners and farmers, who often mine the organic matter from the soil and then rely on chemical fertilizers, out of necessity, Eastern gardeners have recycled nutrients for eons. In fact, they are responsible for developing some of the techniques gardeners refer to collectively as intensive gardening.

When I started gardening in the 1960s, sterile, flat soils supplemented with chemical fertilizers and broad-spectrum pesticides were de rigueur. Trained as an environmentalist and a horticulturist, I questioned these tech-

niques, and by the late 1970s I was a strong advocate of recycling, composting, raised beds, and organic fertilizers and pest controls. Always on the lookout for others of like mind, in the early 1980s I visited with Peter Chan, who gardened at that time in Portland, Oregon. Peter had long been a proponent of an intensive style of vegetable gardening, which he covered in detail in his book *Better Vegetable Gardens the Chinese Way*. Raised in China and trained in agriculture there, Peter wrote of cultural techniques used in China for centuries, including the raised-bed system that promotes good drainage, supplementing soil with organic matter, and composting. Comparing notes with Peter, I found I had instinctively been using numerous time-proven Chinese gardening techniques.

The gardens described in this book, and many of the gardening techniques described in the Appendices, were primarily grown in the Chinese manner—methods now accepted by many modern gardeners worldwide. In addition, I include information on growing greens in what is called the cut-and-come-again method. (See the discussion of my stir-fry garden on page 11 for details.) While not widely practiced in Asia, this method fits right in, as it takes advantage of small spaces.

When I first became interested in Asian vegetables, I was most drawn to Chinese varieties and cooking methods, and I still find them a great place to start for beginners and for gardeners in cooler climates. But in the last decade the gardens and cooking of

Southeast Asia have caught my fancy and I now also experiment with Thai chiles and basils, Vietnamese coriander, lemon grass, and cilantro, among others. Most of these plants are perennials, and while finally becoming more available in nurseries, as they are native to warm climates they are less hardy; most gardeners, including myself, must bring them in over the winter. While they can be a challenge, they are well worth the effort.

The following sections detail both cool-season and warm-season gardens. Most are in my northern California USDA Zone 9 garden, but David Cunningham's Vermont garden offers time-proven techniques for growing in a colder climate. In "The Encyclopedia of Asian Vegetables," I give copious information on growing all the vegetables in the coldest climates as well as in the semitropical regions, where some of the specialties of Southeast Asia will do especially well. For detailed soil preparation, composting, crop rotation, starting from seeds, transplanting, maintenance, and pest-control information, see Appendices A and B.

A typical Asian harvest *(right)* includes Asian eggplants, pac choi, bitter melon, and shallots.

Creasy asian gardens

I live in an unusually good climate for growing cool-season (fall, winter, and spring) vegetables, but it is only so-so for warm-season ones. My garden is in USDA Zone 9, about twenty-five miles from the Pacific Ocean—even less from the San Francisco Bay. The marine influence means winter temperatures seldom sink into the low twenties, with daytime averaging in the fifties. In summer, often the fog doesn't burn off until midmorning, daytime temperature averages in the high seventies, and most nights are in the high fifties. The moderate winter temperatures are perfect for peas, carrots, root vegetables, greens, and all members of the cabbage family, but summer temperatures are borderline for peppers, eggplants, yard-long beans, and some semitropical herbs.

Over the years, I've experimented with hundreds of Asian varieties of vegetables, growing them in small beds by themselves or tucking individual plants in among my lettuces, beans, and tomatoes, but I became inspired to grow a whole garden of Asian vegetables over a twelve-month period, all done specifically for this book.

To give the gardens the feel of Asia, I used bamboo for fencing and trellises and selected rice straw for the paths. The plants were grown in straight rows, which is typical of most Asian gardens, and the beds were raised and formed into geometric patterns. I moved my decades-old Japanese maple into the garden for a focal point, and Edith Shoor, an accomplished ceramist, provided some of her Asian-style pottery for decorative touches here and there. The process was great fun and it entirely transformed my front-yard vegetable garden.

I have incredibly good soil. Of course I should. After twenty years of adding organic mulches and lots of loving care—such as never walking on the beds, planting cover crops, and adding chicken manure from my "ladies" every year—I can dig a hole using only my bare hands.

Shown in the photo to the right are some typical Asian ingredients: Winter melon; Southeast Asian green and white and yellow round, and long purple eggplants; lemon grass; luffa; white bitter melons; and bitter melon vines. One of many Creasy cool-season, frontyard gardens is shown on the opposite page, above. Snow peas are trained on string tepees and Shanghai pac choi and tatsai are growing in the front bed. The harvest from the garden *(opposite, below)* includes snow peas, Japanese red mustard, leek flowers leaves, and pac chois.

The Creasy Cool-Season Vegetable Garden

In late August, my crew and I started seeds of pac choi, mustards, and golden celery in flats to transplant into the garden. In late September, the seeds of snow and pea shoot peas, coriander, fava beans, daikons, Japanese varieties of carrots and spinach, shungiku greens, and bunching onions were all planted directly in the garden. We had good germination on all of the plants, but the slugs went after the coriander seedlings and they needed replanting three times. All went well until January, when we had seven nights in a row that went down to 23°F. Now that's real cold for us Californians and the fava beans burned back to the ground and some of the half-grown pea plants were so weakened we took them out. The cold weather continued into April (March was the coldest on record, with few days climbing out of the forties) and the whole garden was almost a month behind. But it's amazing how resilient cool-season plants are. The fava beans completely recovered and, in fact, produced six or seven stalks instead of the usual three; by early March, the mustards, carrots, onions, daikons, and many greens had revived from their sad-looking state and were producing beautifully. Most of the mustards and

the pac choi were played out and the bunching onions were gone by mid-March. Baby turnips, different greens, and new onions were planted to fill in the beds before the summer crops could be planted.

Stir-fries with gai lon, snow peas, and carrots, and dumpling soups with pac choi and mustards were favorite dishes in my house. I had never made them with pea shoots or with gai lon before, and they are great. New to me were the daikons, shungiku greens, and burdock. As I don't especially enjoy radishes, I was pleasantly surprised to experience their mild, almost sweet taste in a pork soup my neighbor, Helen Chang, taught me to make, and I

enjoyed the daikon pickles made with carrots as well. Helen also showed me how to cook fava beans in the Chinese manner by stir-frying them with garlic and letting visitors peel their own beans as a snack, making them easy to prepare. The shungiku greens were lovely made with a sesame dressing and their flowers created a smoky, mild tea. The burdock was great in a beef roll; I plan to grow it again next year to explore more recipes that feature it. In all, the garden expanded my Asian repertoire. Next winter, I am sure to plant more daikons and fava beans. This garden almost made winter so great I will look forward to the cool temperatures. Well, maybe that's an overstatement.

Another Creasy cool-season Asian garden is shown opposite, above. In November, the beds in my USDA Zone 9 garden are filled with seedlings of mustards, daikons, pac chois, and Japanese carrots ready for thinning. A few months later *(opposite, below)*, the beds are ready for harvesting. The cool-season garden in May is pictured on this page. The fava beans on the left are starting to produce, the snow peas and spinach are in full production, the mizuna is in full bloom and attracting beneficial insects by the drove; and a second planting of greens is ready for harvest.

Plants in the Cool-Season Creasy Asian Garden

Bunching onion: 'Evergreen'

Burdock: 'Takinogawa'

Carrot: 'Japanese Kuroda,' 'Tokita's Scarlet'

Celery: 'Chinese Golden'

Chinese chives: 'Chinese Leek Flower'

Chinese kale: 'Blue Star,' 'Green Delight'

Coriander: 'Slo-Bolt'

Daikon: 'Mino Early,' 'Red Meat'

Gai lon

Japanese onion: 'Kuronobori'

Mizuna

Mustard: 'China Takana,' 'Osaka Purple'

Mustard spinach: 'Komotsuna'

Pac choi: 'Mei Qing,' Tatsoi

Peas: 'Snow Pea Shoots'

Shungiku: 'Round Leaf'

Snow peas: 'Sopporo Express'

Spinach: 'Tamina Asian'

Turnips: 'Market Express'

The Pleasures of a Stir-fry Garden

In the early 1960s, if you were interested in cooking, Cambridge, Massachusetts was a great place to be. Two of this country's doyennes of cuisine held court there: Julia Child and Joyce Chen. Both were filming television shows, and Joyce, author of *The Joyce Chen Cook Book*, was teaching Chinese cooking classes at her restaurant. Living there, I caught the bug and I learned everything—from folding wontons to making béarnaise sauce. From Joyce, I learned one of the most valuable cooking skills you can acquire—how to stir-fry—which became especially pertinent years later, when I became a demon vegetable gardener. Vegetables are the stars of most stir-fries. As a bonus, the recipes are easily varied; one tablespoon of peas or a cup, it seldom matters.

Many years later, after having moved to California, the impetus for creating a specific stir-fry garden was set in motion. I shared a small, sunny part of my garden with a young neighbor, Sandra Chang. As fall approached, it occurred to us, as her mother, Helen, and I used much of my harvest for stir-frying, and so many Asian vegetables grow best in cool weather, that a garden of all stir-fry vegetables would be fun.

Together we chose 'Joi Choi,' a full-size, vigorous pac choi; 'Dwarf Gray' snow peas and 'Sugar Snap' peas; spinach; tatsoi and 'Mei Qing' dwarf pac choi; onions; carrots; cilantro; shungiku; 'Shogun' broccoli, and a stir-fry mix from Shepherd's Garden Seeds containing many different mustards and pac choi. (Winters here seldom go below 28°F; gardeners in cold winter areas would do best to plant these vegetables in early spring.) I planted no

Chinese cabbages, however; mine always become infested with army worms and root maggots.

We started seeds of broccoli and pac choi in August in a flat and direct-seeded the peas in the garden in September. My garden beds are rich with organic matter, so all we added was blood meal before planting. We had extra seeds of many of the greens, so we planted them in containers and grew them on my back retaining wall to see how well they would do. (They grew very well—we fertilized them with fish emulsion every four weeks.) The Shepherd stir-fry mix we planted

A close up *(opposite)* of one of the cool-season beds with gobo and Shanghai pac choi to the left of the bird bath and mustard greens and cilantro on the right. A cut-and-come-again bed of stir-fry greens *(below)* is almost ready for harvesting.

in a little square of soil, about three by three feet, using the cut-and-come-again method. We prepared the soil well and broadcast the seeds like grass seeds, covered them lightly with soil, firmed them in place, and watered them in. We kept the bed moist and had great germination. We didn't thin it, and the seedlings grew problem free—except for occasional slugs, which I controlled by making a few nighttime forays with a flashlight. The vegetables were ready for harvesting at about three inches tall. Using scissors, we snipped our way across the bed an inch above the ground, harvesting as much as we needed at a time. We found these baby greens great for salads and added at the last minute to stir-fries. We fertilized the bed with fish emulsion after harvesting and were able to harvest the greens a second time a month later.

The rest of the beds gave us more than enough vegetables for both families to have a stir-fry or two every week for about three months—great meals of carrot and snap pea stir-fries, chicken with broccoli, tatsoi with ginger, mixed greens with mushrooms and garlic, and oh so many more. Since that stir-fry garden, I have grown many smaller versions and still find them among the most satisfying cool-season gardens.

My stir-fry garden produced far more produce than my husband and I could ever use. My friend Henry Tran *(above)* comes by to cut some greens for stir-frying. Helen Chang *(below)* harvests cilantro from the stir-fry garden. A harvest from the Creasy stir-fry garden is shown on the opposite page.

The Creasy Summer Asian Garden

Match was still colder than usual, but time yields to no one and it soon became the moment to start the summer vegetables, like peppers and eggplants, and the basils, and to order some of the Southeast Asian herbs. The seeds were planted in flats and kept on a warming mat a few inches from fluorescent lights. Germination was good and the plants were moved up to four-inch plastic pots in mid-April, but because it was so cold, they were kept under lights for a few weeks more. Finally they were so big they needed to be moved into larger containers and outside into my cold frame. Even April was very cold, so the plants were not put out until mid-May, when nighttime temperatures were finally above 55°F.

The weather remained colder than usual and July was the coolest on record—mostly overcast days in the high 60s. Some of the vegetables did splendidly in spite of the coolness including the squashes and cucumbers, the soybeans, leek flower, and onions. The eggplants and peppers did better in August as the weather improved— many days in the low 80s. However, my eggplants started to show signs of fusarium wilt (leaves randomly turning brown and the stems showing brown rings inside when cut.) They were in full production and it was painful but one by one we needed to pull them out. The yard-long beans, malabar spinach, and bitter melons, which all need hot weather, were still only three feet tall and never did produce. But all was not

lost, by September the baby corn was ready—delicious—the hot peppers were in full production—spicy—and the cucumbers—over productive—and we were giving them away to all the neighbors. The 'Siam Queen' basil, bunching onions, amaranth, and the shisho all did well. And the winter squash 'Autumn Cup' was extremely productive and ran all over the garden.

The squash themselves were rich and sweet.

All in all, the garden was a success but more stressful than most with all the cold weather. When I plant these hot-weather-loving vegetables again, I will start them under plastic hoops so they get more heat and I'll plant my eggplants in containers. As always, the gardening adventure continues.

Plants in the Warm-Season Creasy Asian Garden

Amaranth: 'Green Leaf,' 'Red Leaf'

Basil: Holy, 'Thai'

Bunching onions: 'Deep Purple'

Corn: 'Baby Asian'

Cucumber: 'Kidma,' 'Orient Express,' 'Suhyo'

Eggplant: 'Millionaire,' 'Ping Tong'

Green onions: 'Ishikura'

Luffa: Ridged

Peppers: 'Cayenne,' 'Hot Asian,' 'Santaka'

Shisho: Green leaf

Shisho: Red leaf

Soybeans: 'Maple Leaf'

Yard-long beans: 'Red Seeded,' 'White Seeded'

Winter squash: 'Autumn Cup'

In my back garden *(opposite)* I designed a small herb garden that included the Asian herbs; mioga ginger, Oriental chives, lemon grass, and even a small container of experimental wasabe. (It is real tricky to grow and after a few months is up and has died.) Also in the beds were bush basil and winter savory. Last year's summer Asian garden *(above)* had many successes: the bunching onions, lots of Japanese cucumbers and squashes, Thai and lemon basils, hot peppers, eggplants, and leek flowers. It was not hot enough for my malabar spinach, bitter melons, and yard-long beans to grow large enough to produce much.

the Cunningham garden

David Cunningham lives in Vermont on a beautiful farm that sits on a knoll with a breathtaking view of the countryside. David grew up there, and I couldn't help thinking that he was clearly destined to go into horticulture. We sat down to plan the Asian garden together as soon as I arrived. Though I didn't pay much attention to the information at the time, David mentioned that his mother was a wolf preservationist—and that the garden was encircled by a wolf yard, then surrounded by a field of sheep.

I returned in midsummer to see the garden, and at that time the wolves were much more in evidence. In fact, to visit the garden we had to exchange places with them; the two wolves went into the house while we went to the garden. Though the idea of being in close proximity to them unnerved me a bit, the wolves were actually quite lovable and shy.

In the garden, which is protected by an electric fence to keep out the wolves, David's horticultural skills were abundantly

manifest. The soil was beautiful—crumbly and dark—and obviously well cared for, and row upon row of healthy Asian vegetables attested to its quality. David told me that long ago the soil had been clay based but that in the early 1950s it started receiving care as a vegetable garden. In winter, the area is planted with winter rye, which in spring is grazed by sheep, and over the years the soil has been amended with mulches and compost. A few years earlier, David had incorporated twenty-five bales of peat moss into the plot. Always careful about keeping the soil healthy, the Cunninghams have kept planks on the paths to avoid packing down the soil because they plan to use it for beds in the future.

The overall vegetable garden is about thirty by forty feet in size, and David had planted a little less than half with Asian vegetables. We started reviewing the garden at the north end, which was planted with three varieties of edible-podded peas: 'Dwarf Gray Sugar,' 'Mammoth

Melting,' and 'Oregon Sugar Pod.' "If I had to pick a favorite," David told me, "I think it would be 'Dwarf Gray Sugar,' because it's such a vigorous grower. It has reddish-purple flowers and the pods are very tasty. At one point, I thought I was going to lose all the peas, because we had a week of temperatures topping 90. All the varieties looked pretty sad for a while, but they perked right up again after it cooled down."

David went on to describe the six varieties of cabbage-type greens he had planted in the next few rows. 'Pac Choy' has white stems, an open form, and doesn't make heads. 'Tyfon,' a cross between Chinese cabbage and turnips, has a mild mustard-like flavor that, according to David, is good in salads. 'Spring A-1' is a cabbage with a medium-tight head and 'WR 90' an upright cabbage with a very tight head. 'Winter Queen' is a cabbage good for fall harvest, and 'Tat Tsai' is a dark green non-heading plant with spoon-shaped leaves growing out of its base.

In the next rows, David had planted the Japanese herb mitsuba, an aromatic parsleylike herb, and 'Green Lance,' a Chinese type of broccoli that David likes using in stir-fries. The head of this broccoli is open and the plant's stem is mainly what is eaten. He had also planted two types of mustard: 'Red Giant,' a striking, somewhat spicy vegetable, and 'Savanna' mustard spinach, a mild-flavored green. The variety of daikon in the garden was 'April Cross.' David described it as very

David Cunningham harvests cabbage from his Asian garden.

tender and uniform with no pith, woodiness, or hollowness. "When you start eating it," he said, "it doesn't seem hot, but it builds up. We eat it in stir-fries, but we've had it raw in salads to and are really happy with it."

David was about to start his fall garden during my visit and was so pleased with the summer's experiment that he wanted to try more varieties of the cabbages. This time he was planning to plant 'Green Rocket,' 'Tsoi Sim,' and 'Taisai' plus shungiku greens and a mustard spinach called 'Osome.'

I asked David about pest problems, and he told me he had had flea beetles on some of the daikon plants and greens and an occasional problem with moles. He remarked that at one time the family had had problems with occasional rabbits, deer, and woodchucks and a serious struggle with raccoons whenever corn was growing. "But," he added, in what I considered a masterful understatement, "since the wolves have been here, things have settled down a bit."

I left this Vermont pastoral scene with my concern about the adaptability of at least some Asian plants put to rest. Many of these wonderful vegetables could be well adapted to a non-Asian kitchen, and David was obviously enjoying both growing and cooking with them. In fact, as far as I was concerned, a fair number of these vegetables had passed the true cooking gardener's test, as David was interested enough to try even more varieties the next season.

the encyclopedia
of asian
vegetables

Asia encompasses diverse climates, from northern China to tropical Thailand, so it is not surprising that Asian vegetables and herbs are an extremely varied lot. For the sake of practicality, I have concentrated here on the vegetables and herbs especially identified with the cuisines of Asia. The majority of species covered are Chinese, Japanese, and Southeast Asian, but I certainly could not discuss Asia without mentioning vegetable favorites from India, Korea, and the Philippines.

Japanese cooks long for mitsuba and green daikon. Thai gardeners, to have a taste of home, must cultivate their own coriander for its roots. Chinese cooks seek out blanched Asian chives,

Shanghai flat cabbage, and an amaranth called Chinese spinach. To enjoy these vegetables and herbs, they usually need to grow their own.

Owing to space limitations, numerous vegetables such as celtuce, taro, and cucuzzi (a type of squash) are not covered here but are well worth exploring, as are other seasonings such as turmeric, galangal, and many Japanese herbs, which are not reliably available commercially as plants.

The format of the entries calls for a

few words of explanation. Each vegetable is listed under its most common English name, followed by alternate common names in parentheses, the Latin name, and the Asian name(s), where pertinent. Regarding the spelling of Chinese names there is great confusion, primarily because the English words are transliterated from Chinese characters. The result is a diversity of spellings approximating the original sounds. Pac choi, for example, might also be spelled *pak choy*, *bok choy*, *bok choi*, and *baak choi*. I have chosen to use the North American spellings.

A number of seed companies carry Asian varieties of vegetables and herbs; these are listed on page 102. The largest offerings are available from Evergreen Y. H. Enterprises and Kitazawa Seed Company, which specialize in Asian vegetables.

An Asian harvest includes: 'Japanese Giant Red' mustard, 'Joi Choi,' tatsoi, mibuna, leek flowers, and snow and 'Sugar Snap' peas.

'Merah' amaranth

AMARANTH

(CHINESE SPINACH; LEAF AMARANTH) AMARANTHUS TRICOLOR

(A. gangeticus, A. mangostanus)
Hindi: *chaulai;* **Mandarin:** *xian cai;*
Cantonese: *yin choi;* **Japanese:** *hi-yu-na*

AMARANTH IS A NEW WORLD plant that has been enjoyed for centuries in Asia, where the leaf type is preferred to the grain types. In parts of China, a variety with green and red leaves is popular; in India, cooks select the light green.

Most leaf amaranths grow to 18 inches and are best when the leaves are young and tender.

How to grow: Amaranth, a tropical annual, glories in warm weather. Start seedlings after all danger of frost has passed. Plant seeds $1/8$ inch deep and 4 inches apart in full sun and rich, well-drained soil. Either grow the plants as a cut-and-come-again crop, harvested when only a few inches tall (see "The Pleasures of a Stir-fry Garden" for information on page 11) or thin the plants to 1 foot apart and grow full-sized plants. Keep amaranth fairly moist. Generally, amaranth grows with great enthusiasm. Cucumber beetles are occasionally a problem.

Harvest by hand, selecting the young, tender leaves and shoots. If growing as a cut-and-come-again crop, harvest with scissors as needed.

Varieties

Green Leaf Amaranth: 50 days; pointed, oval, dark green leaves; popular in subtropical areas

'Merah': 80 days; crinkled green and red leaves

'Puteh': 80 days, mild, light green leaves

White Leaf Amaranth: light green leaves; dwarf plants popular in Taiwan and Japan

How to prepare: Amaranth should be cooked only briefly, as it gets mushy. Popular ways to cook it are by stir-frying or adding it to soup made with pork and garlic. According to chef Ken Hom, "Westerners usually cut the stems off, but most Chinese love the texture, even though the stems are kind of stringy." He likes amaranth simply stir-fried and flavored with fermented bean curd (also known as tempeh).

BAMBOO

Bambusa spp. (clumping bamboo) and *Phyllostachys* spp. (running bamboo)

Chinese: *mo sun* **(spring shoots),** *jook sun* **(summer shoots),** *doeng sun* **(winter shoots); Japanese:** *takenoko;* **Indonesian:** *rebung;* **Malaysian:** *rebung;* **Tagalog:** *labong;* **Thai:** *normai;* **Vietnamese:** *mang*

BAMBOO IS ONE OF THE MOST useful and beloved plants in Asia. The young shoots are cooked and included in many dishes. The familiar canned product is tinny tasting and flaccid when compared to fresh shoots.

For the gardener, there are two types of bamboo: clumping and running. Running bamboo does run-it can even come up through asphalt. See the following growing instructions for how to contain running bamboo. The clumping type stays confined, sending up only basal stems.

How to grow: Bamboos are perennial grasses. Most are semihardy, but a few are hardy in the 0°F range. All species prefer well-drained, rich loam with a high organic content. In hot-summer areas, bamboo needs some shade, in cool coastal areas, full sun. During the first few years, fertilize with a balanced organic fertilizer in spring and midsummer. Thereafter, the dropped leaves and a yearly application usually suffice. Most bamboos are drought tolerant but produce the tenderest shoots when watered well. Newly established plants must not be allowed to dry out. To protect new shoots in winter, mulch well or, if bamboo is in a container, bring it into a well-lit room. Check occasionally, as bamboo litter sometimes prevents water from penetrating the root area during rain. Thin out three-year-old canes and use them for trellises, staking, and fencing. Bamboo has no major pests or diseases. To prevent bamboo itself from becoming a pest, make sure the roots of the running types are contained within a concrete or metal barrier at least 2 feet deep, or plant it in containers.

New shoots of the clumping bamboos usually appear in summer or fall, the running types in spring. Harvest the large shoots just as they emerge by freeing them from soil and, with a sturdy, sharp knife, cut off the top 6 to 8 inches. (If you make 6-inch mounds of soil around the base of the plant before the shoots emerge, they will be

Grove of giant bamboo *(below left)*, and narrow bamboo shoots, ready for harvest *(below right)*

Giant bamboo shoots, peeled *(above)*, and how to cut the small-diameter shoots *(below)*

easier to harvest and the shoots will be longer.) The more slender species, generally referred to as summer bamboos, produce shoots 1–2 inches wide. These can be allowed to grow to a height of 12 inches before being harvested at ground level. In all cases, do not harvest all the shoots; the plants need to renew themselves.

Varieties

In this case, the term *varieties* refers to the species described in the following list. All bamboos produce shoots; a few specially recommended ones are listed below.

Upper Bank Nurseries and Bamboo Sourcery offer many types, including some of the species recommended below. Bamboos are often available locally as well.

Bambusa beecheyana (**Beecheyana Bamboo):** clumping type; 15 feet tall; stems 4 inches wide; hardy to USDA Zone 9; graceful form

Bambusa glaucescens (**Hedge Bamboo):** clumping type; 20 feet tall; 1 1/2 inches wide; hardy to USDA Zone 8

Phyllostachys aurea (**Golden Bamboo):** running type; 15 feet tall; stems 2 inches wide; hardy to USDA Zone 7

P. dulce (**Sweet Shoot):** running type; 30 feet tall; stems 2 1/2 inches wide; hardy to USDA Zone 8; considered the sweetest shoots

P. nuda: running type; 35 feet tall; stems 1 1/2 inches wide; hardy to USDA Zone 5, among the hardiest types

P. heterocycla pubescens (P. edulis) (**Moso):** running type; 50 feet tall; stems 6 inches wide; hardy to USDA Zone 7

How to prepare: For the large, thick bamboo shoots, cut a ring around the outside of the bottom of the shoot with a knife and peel the first outer layer to expose the white flesh; repeat this procedure for a dozen or so layers until all the brown leaves are removed and the shoot is white. Then, as you would with asparagus, if the base is tough, remove that as well. Cut the shoot in very thin slices.

The small-diameter shoots must also be peeled; in this case, remove the outer layer between each joint, one joint at a time. Slice the shoots in rings and discard the woody joints.

If the shoots are sweet (which is the exception), they can be eaten raw in salads. However, most shoots are fairly tough and have a bitter taste that must be removed by parboiling for 20 minutes. Change the water after the first 10 minutes and drain the shoots when you are done parboiling. Taste the shoots and, if they are still bitter, repeat the process. After parboiling, the slices can be used in any recipe calling for bamboo shoots or frozen in plastic freezer bags.

To serve immediately, cook until tender. The most popular use of bamboo is in stir-fried dishes. Bamboo shoots are most popular in northern China, where they are used in soups, stews, dumplings, noodle and meat dishes, meat and vegetable stir-fries, and, often, with mushrooms or pickled mustard (see recipe, page 65). For example, bamboo is used in gai lon with barbecued pork (see recipe, page 72), spring rolls with Chinese chives and shredded pork, and Thai beef with bamboo shoots. In Japan, fresh bamboo shoots are occasionally grilled on skewers and glazed with soy sauce or miso, or used in braised vegetable dishes. Of course, they can be used in any recipe calling for canned shoots.

BASILS

THAI BASIL

Ocimum basilicum
Thai: *bai horapa;* **Vietnamese:** *rau que*

LEMON BASIL
O. citriodorum
Thai: *bai manglak*

HOLY BASIL
O. sanctum
Hindi: *tulsi;* **Thai:** *bai gaprow*

'Siam Queen' *(above);* Holy basil *(left);* Lemon basil *(right)*

THREE ASIAN BASILS ARE prominent ingredients in the cuisines of Southeast Asia. Red-stemmed Thai basil is relatively similar in taste and appearance to Italian sweet basil, but with an anise flavor. Small-leafed lemon basil has a delicate citrus scent and taste. Purple-tinged holy basil, with slightly serrated leaves, has a strong scent of cloves and a musky taste. Holy basil is so named because it is sacred to the Hindu gods and is found planted near temples and homes in India.

How to grow: Basils are annuals that glory in hot weather and wither in the frost. Gardeners in cool-summer areas struggle to keep them going. Choose a well-drained area of the garden in full sun or light shade, and with fertile organic soil.

You can start basil seeds inside a month before planting them out, or purchase them as transplants from specialty nurseries in the spring. Basil put out in the garden before the weather is warm suffers badly. Space seedlings 1 foot apart. Keep the plants fairly moist during the growing season. Feed basil with fish emulsion every 6 weeks and after a large harvest.

Harvest basil leaves about 80 days from sowing by picking or cutting. Keep the flower heads continually cut back or the plant will go to seed.

Varieties

Seeds of Thai, lemon, and holy basil can be purchased from the herb catalogs listed in Resources. 'Siam Queen' is a new variety of Thai basil that is compact and tasty.

How to prepare: Thai basil is excellent in Southeast Asian curries of vegetables, chicken, and game (see recipe, page 86). Both Thai basil and lemon basil are excellent for flavoring soups and added fresh to salads. The seeds of lemon basil are used in sweet drinks and mixed with coconut milk to make a dessert. Soaked in drinks, these seeds become slippery, yet crunchy. In Vietnam and Thailand, lemon and Thai basils are combined on a platter with fresh mints, Vietnamese coriander or cilantro, and lettuce to put in spring rolls, which are served with a spicy dip (see recipe, page 78.)

Holy basil is almost always used in noodle dishes paired with chicken or shellfish. Use this basil according to taste, for its flavor intensifies in cooking.

BEANS

ADZUKI (RED BEAN)
Vigna angularis
Mandarin: *hong xiao dou, chi dou;*
Japanese: *azuki*

MUNG (GREEN BEAN)
V. radiata
Chinese: *look dow*

SOY (SOYA BEAN, SOYBEAN)
Glycine max
Mandarin: *da dou;* **Cantonese:** *tai tau,*
wong tau, hak tau; **Japanese:** *daizu,*
eda mame

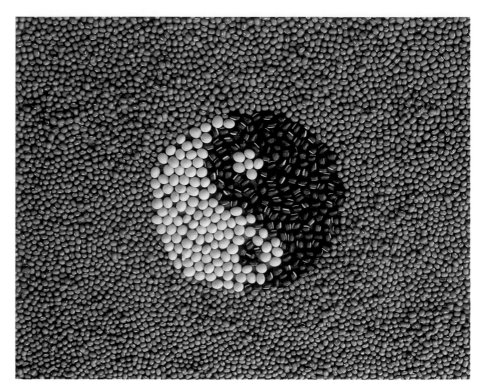

A layout of green mung, white soy, and red adzuki beans.

ADZUKI BEANS ARE POPULAR in Japan. The pods, which grow to about 4 inches, contain reddish seeds; the flowers are rose colored. Mung beans have purplish yellow flowers, hairy pods that grow to about 4 inches, and green seeds. Both are bushy plants that reach about 3 feet tall. Soybeans are a powerhouse of nutrition and the major source of protein for many Asians. The white- and black-seeded ones are generally used as dry beans, the green-seeded ones for fresh eating. Soybean plants have fuzzy leaves, stems, and pods and grow to about 2 feet. The tiny flowers are white or lilac.

How to grow: Soy, adzuki, and mung beans are all annuals, grown much as you would regular bush beans. Plant after all danger of frost is past and the soil has warmed to at least 60°F. Plant in full sun in a well-drained garden loam. Sow seeds 1 inch deep in rows 24 inches apart. Thin seedlings to 4 inches apart. (Wider spacing is needed for soybeans in southern areas.) Once established, water deeply and infrequently. If the plants look pale at midseason, fertilize with fish emulsion.

The Mexican bean beetle can be a pest in certain areas. Phytophthora can be a problem for soybeans, especially in overly moist soil.

You can eat the immature pods of both adzuki and mung beans or let them mature and use the beans fresh shelled or dried. Harvest soybeans for fresh shelling when the pods are plump but still green or let them dry before harvesting. If letting the beans dry on the plant, harvest after the plant turns brown. Pull up the whole plant and hang to dry completely in a warm, dry place. Shell the beans and store them in airtight containers in a cool, dry place.

Varieties

Mung and Adzuki Varieties

Mung and adzuki beans are usually not available as named varieties. Vermont Bean Seed Company and Evergreen Y. H. Enterprises carry them.

Adzuki: 60 days pods, 90 days mature seeds; high yields; pods contain 7–10 beans

Mung: 90 days mature; pods contain 7–9 beans; use for plants or sprouting if not treated with fungicides

Soybean Varieties

Johnny's Select Seeds, Evergreen Y. H. Enterprises, and Kitazawa Seed Company carry a few varieties.

'Butterbeans': 90 days, fresh; green beans, buttery flavor; high yields, good fresh

'Envy': 75 days, fresh; very early, short-season favorite; green beans good fresh or dried

Soybean plants *(above)*; soybeans *(below)*

[How to Sprout Mung and Soybeans]

It is amazingly easy to sprout bean seeds, which can be a fun project for children. Purchase seeds in bulk from an Asian grocery or a health-food store, or order sprouting seeds from a mail-order nursery. When obtaining them from a nursery, make sure the seeds have not been treated with a fungicide that is applied to aid sprouting in cold soils.

Of the several ways to sprout beans, the easiest is to put $^1/_2$ cup of seeds in a clean 1-quart widemouthed mason jar and cover the top of the jar with cheesecloth tied with string. Soak the bean seeds in water overnight and drain them the next morning. Put the jar in a cool, dark place, like a closet, to sprout. Rinse the seeds with cold water 2 to 3 times a day to cool the growing sprouts and provide moisture (more often in warm weather). Drain them well each time. Repeat the process for 4 or 5 days or until the seeds have sprouted and are about 1 $^1/_2$ inches long. Once the sprouts are ready, rinse them well to remove most of the hulls and refrigerate them. The sprouts deteriorate quickly and are best used within a day. Your mung and soy sprouts will be curlier and a little smaller than those grown commercially, but they taste the same. One word of caution: Soybean sprouts need to be cooked before they are eaten.

Soy, Verde: 98 days; not for northern climates; very nutty flavor; 3-foot bushes with pea-sized green beans

How to prepare: Green soybeans can be cooked in numerous ways when fresh or allowed to mature and used as dry beans. Add raw fresh beans to raw rice and cook them together, as they cook up at the same rate.

The great majority of white soybeans in Asia are made into soy prod-ucts or consumed as sprouts. The latter use is particularly prevalent in Cantonese dishes, where they are stir-fried or used in soups. In Korea, the sprouts are used for salads (see recipe, page 78), and in a stew with pork. (**Caution:** Soy sprouts are not edible in their raw state and are always eaten cooked.) The Japanese enjoy the fresh green soybeans in a traditional fall snack (edamame) consumed with beer. The beans, pod and all (sometimes still on the stalk), are boiled in salted water and drained; then snackers shell their own, as we do peanuts in the shell (see recipe, page 82). In Japan, the beans are sometimes shelled and added raw to rice before it is cooked (see recipe, page 66).

Adzuki are widely used in Asia for soups, but especially in desserts, and in a sweet paste for dumplings. The young pods are eaten like snow peas.

Mung bean sprouts are one of the most widely used vegetables in stir-fries in general, in various classic Asian stir-fries with pork, and in sweet-and-sour soup.

BEANS, FAVA
(BROAD BEANS)
Vicia faba
Chinese: *tsaam dou;* **Hindi:** *bakla;*
Japanese: *sora mame*

BEANS, YARD-LONG
(ASPARAGUS BEAN; CHINESE PEA)
Vigna unguiculata spp. Sesquipedalis
Cantonese: *cheung kong tau;* **Mandarin:** *chang dou;* **Japanese:** *sasage*

PIGEON PEAS (RED GRAM, DAHL)
Cajanus cajan

FAVAS ARE COOL-SEASON BEANS, good for cool climates. On the other hand, yard-long beans and pigeon peas are best grown in warm climates.

Yard-long beans produce very long, thin pods. These vining plants, which are related to black-eyed peas, grow to 10 feet. The young pods, seeds, and leaves are edible. The pod and foliage flavor is mild and sweet. There are three types of yard-long beans: the dark, thin pods with black seeds; the larger, light green one with spongy pods and red seeds; and a white-seeded type.

Pigeon peas are shrubby perennials from Asia and Africa that are popular in east Indian cuisine. The quick-growing plants can be 9 feet tall and 6 feet wide.

How to grow: In areas where winters don't dip below the teens, plant

Fava bean flowers *(above)*, fava bean pods *(below)*

fava beans in the fall. They need about 90 days of cool weather and tolerate repeated frosts. In cold-winter areas, plant favas when you plant peas. To plant, prepare the soil well and plant seeds 2 inches deep and about 3 inches apart. The plants grow quickly to 5 feet in height. Support the tall plants with stakes and strings surrounding

the outsides of the beds. Black aphids sometimes infest fava beans; control them with sprays of water. Slugs can destroy seedling beds. For young, tender fava beans whose skins do not need to be removed, harvest them when they first start to fill out the pods. Alternately, let the fava beans mature and use them fresh or dried.

Yard-long beans are hot-weather annuals that produce poorly in cool-summer areas. Plant them in full sun at least 2 weeks after your last expected frost, sowing the seeds 1 inch deep and 4 inches apart. Thin the seedlings to 8 inches. Make successive plantings 3 weeks apart. Yard-long beans need trellising and produce best if kept fairly moist. Fertilize sparingly—too much nitrogen results in few beans. Pest and disease problems are minimal. Harvest when pods reach 12 to 18 inches, before the seeds fill out the pods.

Pigeon peas are tender tropical shrubs that need a very long, warm growing season. They tolerate poor soils. Plant 1/2 inch deep and 5 feet apart. The plants may need support. In Florida, the plants produce for up to 5 years if there are no freezes. Harvest pods while young or let them mature and harvest the seeds for drying.

Varieties

Fava Beans

'Nintoku Giant': three large green seeds per pod; grows well in warmer climates

'Windsor': 80 days; bush; grows to 4 feet with green pods to 10 inches; large, light green beans

Yard-Long Beans

Redwood City Seed and Evergreen Y. H. Enterprises both carry yard-long beans.

Red Seeded: 75 days; heirloom; light green pods; maroon brown seeds; trouble-free variety

Black Seeded: the most widely grown yard-long; dark green pods

Black Stripe Seed: new variety from Taiwan; high yields; pods are crisp

'Kaohsiung': dark green, thick, meaty pods and black seeds

'Sabah Snake': 80 days; very long pods; pods are light green and wrinkled; white seeds; heirloom; popular in Malaysia

Pigeon Peas

ECHO and The Banana Tree carry pigeon pea seeds.

Yard-long beans *(above)*, pigeon peas *(below)*

How to prepare: Young fava beans have a special sweetness. These tasty beans are shelled when the seeds start to fill out the pods. Then the bean skins must be peeled before preparation—double peeling—a real labor of love. In northern China, the beans are paired with ham or sprouted and cooked. In parts of China and Japan, mature fresh fava beans are parboiled, then stir-fried in a little oil and garlic. Diners eat them as a snack, peeling the skins off themselves.

Caution: Some males of Mediterranean descent are allergic to favas and should be wary when trying them for the first time; persons taking antidepressants with monoamine inhibitors should avoid them at all costs.

Yard-long beans are actually tastiest when 12–18 inches long. In a popular Szechwan dish called dry-fried beans, the red-seeded yard-long beans are deep-fried, drained, and then put in a wok and stir-fried with spicy seasonings. The dark green variety is best in a simple stir-fry with a bit of ginger. Try them in rolls of marinated beef or pork (see recipe, page 81) or add them to soups. These beans are pencil-thin and a bit like French haricots verts; they can be used in place of string beans in most recipes.

The young pods of pigeon peas are eaten cooked, or the fresh or dried seed is cooked and eaten, often with rice. In the Philippines, pigeon peas are often used in soups (see recipe, page 74.)

Bitter melon

BITTER MELON
(BITTER GOURD; BITTER CUCUMBER; BALSAM PEAR)
Momordica charantia
Cantonese: *fu kwa;* **Mandarin:** *ku gwa;*
Japanese: *niga uri;* **Hindi:** *karela*

BITTER MELONS ARE WARTY vegetables that somewhat resemble their cousins the cucumber and have a distinctive, quininelike taste. They are popular in Asia where bitter tastes are appreciated. In the Philippines, the juice from a bitter melon is sometimes rubbed on babies' lips to accustom children to bitter tastes. The immature leaves and shoots are edible, too.

Bitter melon plants are handsome vines that bear yellow flowers and may climb more than 12 feet. The unique fruits may be light or dark green, or white when young; they mature to red orange.

How to grow: Bitter melons are grown as annuals. They need long, warm growing conditions. Soak the seeds for 24 hours before planting to help germination. Start bitter melons inside at a minimum soil temperature of 64°F. Once in the garden, they need full sun and a fertile, organic soil. Space or thin plants to 2 feet apart. Put a trellis in place for them to grow on when you plant them. Bitter melons require ample water.

If the vines are pale at midseason, apply fish emulsion. If the plants are not setting fruit, you need to hand pollinate the flowers. Slugs and snails can be a problem for young plants.

Harvest bitter melons while they are young and still firm, in the white or green stage. They grow more bitter as they mature. Harvest regularly and do not let them ripen on the vine; they will continue to ripen after harvesting. Harvest leaves and shoots for cooking while they are young.

Varieties
In some sources, bitter melons are listed only by the common or species names rather than by variety names.

'High Moon': 90 days; pale green to white; to 10 inches long. Available from Territorial Seed Company

'Hong Kong': dark green, rather smooth skin; spindle shaped; more bitter and flavorful than most; Cantonese use this for stuffing

'Karela': 55 days; dark green, to 7 1/2 inches long; very productive; from India; carried by Willhite Seed Company

'Taiwan Large': large, high-quality fruits, green skin and white flesh; disease resistant; popular in Taiwan

'Thailand': small fruits with blistered, deep green skin; productive; popular in tropics

How to prepare: In much of Asia, bitter melon is considered to have cooling or medicinal properties, and the young tendrils are considered a delicacy and are prepared by quick frying. Alternately, they are incorporated at the last minute into simple egg dishes. The tendrils have some bitterness but possess a distinctive, quite pleasant vegetable taste. The taste of the fruits varies in flavor and bitterness depending on maturity. Most fruits begin deep green and mild and grow increasingly yellow and bitter with age. Try young melons in soups and mature ones in stir-fries (see the recipe on page 70) or stuffed with meat. In China, bitter melon is usually cooked in a soup with pork and black beans or added to stir-fries. In India, bitter melon is often cooked with potatoes and numerous spices or pickled with garlic; it is also fried, stuffed, and used in curries. Before cooking with bitter melon, to remove much of the water and some of the bitterness, slice, salt, and then squeeze the juice out.

BUNCHING ONIONS

(GREEN ONIONS, SCALLIONS, MULTI-PLIER ONIONS, WELSH ONIONS)

Allium fistulosum

Cantonese: *ts'ung fa;* **Mandarin:** *cong* **(onion)**, *quing cong;* **Japanese:** *negi*

BUNCHING ONIONS ARE bulbless onions widely used throughout Asia. They are hardy perennials and are cultivated for their long, white stems and green leaves. There are two basic types: those that grow as single-stemmed onions and those that are multi-stemmed and grow in clusters. The single-stemmed types are grown as annuals and can be planted quite close together. The clustering types continue to spread from year to year.

How to grow: As with other alliums, bunching onions prefer cool weather and soil rich in organic matter and phosphorous. Plant bunching onions from seed in the spring for summer use or in the fall to overwinter. Sow 1/4 inch apart and 1/2 inch deep. Keep weeded. Give consistent moisture. The clustering types should reach a good size the first year, with some division at the base; they can be divided the second summer. To produce whiter stalks, mound the soil to blanch the stems. The long, single-stalked types are particularly well-suited for blanching and are sometimes called Chinese leeks. Bunching onions are fairly resistant to pests and disease.

Multistemmed bunching onions

Harvest the leaves when young, as you would chives. Once the plants are established, harvest the individual scallions or separate from the cluster as needed.

Varieties

'Evergreen Hardy' ('Evergreen'): 65 days; very popular; grows in clusters; most cold hardy of the bunching onions

'Kujo' ('Kujo Green Multistalk'): a multiplier onion; grows in clusters of 3 or 4 stalks; tender white stalks are about 10 inches long; light green leaves to 18 inches

'Ishikura No. 2': a popular single-stalked variety; very uniform

'White Lisbon': 60 days; an *Allium cepa* developed for use as a scallion; tender green tops and long white stems; does well in a variety of soils

How to prepare: Bunching onions can become bitter if overcooked, so they are generally chopped and added to cooked dishes toward the end of cooking. In China, these green onions are used as garnishes or added to rice, noodle, and fish dishes as well as soups and stir-fries. Historically, the nomadic tribes of Mongolia gathered the wild green onions that grew profusely in that region. They then quickly fried thin strips of beef and added handfuls of the onions at the last minute, the object being to cook the green onions lightly while still keeping the life in them. In Japanese cooking, these onion-family vegetables are widely used for pickling, in soups and garnishes, and are popular in sukiyaki.

Burdock

BURDOCK

Arctium lappa

Cantonese: *ngao pong;* **Mandarin:** *niu pang;* **Japanese:** *gobo*

THIS PLANT'S ROOTS, WHICH can grow to 4 feet long and 1 inch wide, and its young shoots are prized in Japan. The roots are usually brown-skinned with white flesh. The plant grows to about 3 feet tall.

How to grow: Burdock is a biennial but is usually grown as an annual sown in early spring. It can also be sown in the fall and harvested in early spring. Soak the seeds overnight in warm water and then plant in extremely soft, deep, rich soil in full sun. Work in bone meal before planting. Thin seedlings to 8 inches apart. Keep mulched for vigorous growth throughout the season. Harvest the roots in approximately 4 months. The roots are tenderest when harvested while young, at 12 to 18 inches long. The best way to harvest is to use a post-hole digger next to the plant to expose the majority of the root before you pull it out; otherwise the root breaks off easily.

Varieties

'Takinogawa': 120 days; the standard Japanese variety; has well-formed roots with a mild, bittersweet flavor

How to prepare: The primary edible part of burdock is the root, but young, tender shoots are sometimes used too. The roots are sometimes used in stir-fries and soups in China. In Japan, they are pickled or cooked in soups, tempura, and stir-fries with slivered carrots. Try them rolled in thin strips of beef or pork mixed with other vegetables (see recipe, page 81). Roots are harvested and scraped before cooking; stronger-tasting roots are thinly sliced and soaked in water for several hours to remove bitterness. Keep cut roots in water to prevent darkening.

CARROTS

Daucus carota var. sativus
Hindi: *gajar*

CARROTS ARE POPULAR IN India, but plant breeders in Japan and Taiwan have developed many great modern varieties we use in the West. A number of the Asian carrots are high in anthocyanins, which gives them a reddish cast.

How to grow: Plant carrots in early spring, as soon as your soil has warmed, or plant them as a fall crop. Cultivate and loosen the soil 1 foot deep to make room for the roots. Light soils are best—gardeners with heavy soils need stubby varieties. Sow seeds 1/2 inch apart in rows or wide beds and keep the seed bed evenly moist. Thin to 2 inches. In most parts of the country, once sprouted, carrots are easy to grow. When the plants are about 3 inches tall, mulch with compost and side dress with fish emulsion.

Once the seedlings are up, protect them from snails and slugs. In the upper Midwest, the carrot rust fly maggot tunnels its way through carrots. Floating row covers and crop rotation help. Alternaria blight and cercospora blight are possible diseases.

Carrot varieties are ready for harvesting when they are at least 1/2 inch across and start to color. The optimal time to harvest carrots is within a month after they mature, less in very warm weather. Harvest when the soil is moist. To prolong the fall harvest in cold climates, mulch plants well with 1 foot of dry straw and cover with plastic that's weighted down with something heavy.

Varieties

'Carrot Suko' (Baby Carrot): 70 days; very sweet; bred for growing as baby carrots 3 to 4 inches long

'Dragon': 75 days; red to purplish exterior, yellow to orange interior; sweet, spicy flavor; the purplish exterior is high in anthocyanin; available from Garden City

'Kinko': 52 days; very early; 4 to 6 inches long, sweet Japanese carrot; best harvested young

'Kuroda': 90 days; heat tolerant; tender and sweet; 6 to 8 inches long; stores well

'Tokita's Scarlet': 100 days; very sweet; heat resistant, 7 inches long; Japanese

How to prepare: Carrots find their way into numerous dishes in India, including many curries, and they are made into pickles and sweetmeats. The red varieties are more favored in China and are consumed most heavily around the Chinese New Year. Grated carrots are added to a popular Vietnamese salad dressing that includes lemon juice and fish sauce. Koreans add them to kim chee and, traditionally, daikon pickles (see recipe, page 63). In much of Southeast Asia, carrots are carved and used for a garnish.

Japanese carrots

Chinese broccoli

CHINESE BROCCOLI

(CHINESE KALE)

Brassica oleracea var. *alboglabra*

Cantonese: *kaai laan tsoi*;
Mandarin: *gai lan*

CONSIDERED BY MANY TO BE one of the choicest cabbage-family greens, Chinese broccoli, also sold as gai lon, grows rapidly to 18 inches and has blue green leaves, thick stems, and white flowers. While not really a broccoli (it's a kale), the plant is allowed to form buds before it's eaten, so cooks treat it as a broccoli.

How to grow: Chinese broccoli is easier to grow than most of the cabbage family. Sow seed outside in full sun in spring and again in late summer. In cool summer areas, it will pro-

duce over the summer. In mild-winter areas, it grows well as a winter crop if frosts are light. The season can be extended by starting some seeds inside in early spring and by protecting late crops from hard frost. Plant seeds ¼ inch deep in an organic, fertile soil. Thin to about 8 inches apart and keep well watered. The plants need to grow quickly to be tender and mild. Chinese broccoli is fairly pest and disease free, though it can be affected by common cabbage-family problems.

Harvest the flowering stalks just before the buds start to open. Cut the stalks 6 to 8 inches from the top of the plant to force new side growth.

Varieties

'Blue Star': popular in U.S. Chinatowns; the large stems and flower buds are crisp and tender

'Green Delight': slightly smaller than 'Blue Star'; grows well in mild or warm climates

'Green Lance': 50 days; disease resistant

How to prepare: To prepare the stalks for cooking, first peel the stems as you would asparagus, removing any tough skin. Large leaves are tough also; remove these, leaving succulent stems with a small flowering top. Cut these into pieces about 2 to 3 inches long, ready for cooking. While Chinese broccoli is enjoyed in soups with noodles, mushrooms, and pork, squid, or chicken, stir-frying is the most popular way to prepare it. Try it with barbecued pork (see recipe, page 72).

'Michihili' Chinese cabbage

CHINESE CABBAGE

Brassica rapa var. *pekinensis*
Mandarin: *da bai cai*; **Cantonese:** *bok choi*; **Japanese:** *nappa*

CHINESE CABBAGES HAVE milder flavor and tenderer leaves than their cousins, the Western cabbages (which are sometimes grown in the Orient). There are three major types of Chinese cabbages: one is barrel-shaped, light green, and often referred to as napa cabbage; another is tall and cylindrical, with lacy Savoy-type leaves, sometimes referred to as Michihili cabbage; the third is an attractive, loose-headed cabbage.

How to grow: Chinese cabbages can be fussy. They don't transplant well and tend to bolt if disturbed or if subjected to cold temperatures while young. Growing them for fall harvest

Young Chinese cabbage with pine needle mulch

12 inches tall; tender, ruffly leaves; sow late spring through late summer; bolts in cold spring weather

'Michihili': 78 days; open pollinated; cylindrical head 16 inches tall by inches wide; green leaves; for mild climates

'Spring A-1' (Takii's Spring A-1'): 73 days; a bolt resistant, mild, sweet, light green cabbage with 3-pound heads; for spring sowing

'Wong Bok': 90 days, napa type; heads 10 inches tall, 6 inches across; tender; sow in early summer for fall harvest

How to prepare: Cabbage is a staple in much of Asia. In China, these cabbages are most commonly prepared with meat in soups and stir-fries. They absorb flavors well and are often combined with oyster sauce and black bean sauce, garlic, and seafood to be used as a stuffing for potstickers and spring rolls. As for preserving cabbages, there are many techniques. In China, the cabbages are often dried in the sun and used in soups in the winter. Most types are also pickled in brine, brine vinegar, or salt and hot peppers in some areas and served as a condiment or added to meat or tofu stir-fries. See the pickled mustard recipe on page 65 for pickling methods. In Korea, pickled cabbages are the basis for most *kim chee,* a vegetable pickle seasoned with garlic, lots of red peppers, and ginger; it is the national dish. Japanese cooks use Chinese cabbage in soups; in sukiyaki, where it is braised with meat; in shabu-shabu, a one-pot meal cooked at the table; and pickled.

reduces disease and insect problems and decreases the tendency to bolt. Start them from seeds planted directly in the garden about midsummer (2 1/2 to 3 months before your first fall frost) so they mature in the cool weather. A few varieties, designated as spring or slow bolting, can be planted in the spring and harvested in early summer.

Cabbages need a fertile, loamy soil filled with organic matter. They prefer full sun, or light shade in hot climates. Sow the seeds 1/2 inch deep; thin to 12 inches apart. Cabbages are heavy feeders, so add a balanced organic fertilizer: 1 cup worked into the soil around each plant at planting time. Chinese cabbages are shallow rooted and need regular and even watering and a substantial mulch to retain moisture.

Chinese cabbages are susceptible to many pests and diseases. I find the napa types and the pale-leafed varieties seem to get more than their share. Flea beetles, imported cabbageworm, and cut-

worms may be problems. The maggot of the cabbage root fly and aphids are other possible pests. Clubroot is one of the most serious fungus diseases of the cabbage family. Good garden hygiene is imperative. Rotate members of the cabbage family with other vegetable families. Select varieties that are resistant to cabbage diseases. Use floating row covers to protect cabbages from pests.

Harvest Chinese cabbages once the heads feel firm. In the fall, they can tolerate light frost; if a hard freeze is expected, harvest the heading cabbages and store them in a cool place.

Varieties

If direct seeding, as advised, add 2 weeks to the following days-to-maturity numbers.

'Jade Pagoda': 72 days; hybrid; popular Michihili type; 16 inches tall by 6 inches wide; medium green; vigorous; slow bolting

'Lettucy Type': 45 days; tall, open top,

'Chinese Golden' celery

CHINESE CELERY

Apium graveolens
Mandarin: *quing cai*; **Cantonese:** *k'an tsoi*; **Japanese:** *seri-na*; **Thai:** *kin chai*

CHINESE CELERY IS A CLOSE relative of the celery commonly enjoyed in the West. It has thin, hollow stems and is a smaller, hardier plant than the more familiar variety.

How to grow: Like its Western relative, Chinese celery is a biennial grown as a cool-season annual. Chinese celery grows best as a spring or fall crop. It needs full sun (or partial shade in hot areas) and a highly organic, fertile soil that retains moisture well. Start seeds indoors 8 weeks before planting outdoors. After the weather has warmed, move seedlings into the garden and place them 1 foot apart. Seeds can also be started outside in the seed bed. Fertilize the plants with liquid fish emulsion every month and keep the soil continually moist.

As a rule, Chinese celery is subject to few pests and diseases, though leaf miners can cause problems.

Some gardeners elect to garden blanch their celery. This produces stalks with a more delicate flavor. To blanch: After the plants start to mature, exclude light for about 3 weeks by wrapping the stalks with burlap or straw; surround the bundles with black plastic and tie them with string.

Harvest stems when they are about 10 inches high. New stalks will continue to form. Alternately, harvest the whole head by cutting the plant off at the ground with a sharp knife.

Varieties

In some sources, this plant is listed simply as Chinese celery.
'Chinese Golden': yellowish green stems and leaves; small leaves; resistant to cold temperatures
'Green Queen': deep green stems and leaves; tender and flavorful

How to prepare: Chinese celery is a staple in many Asian soups and stews. It is stronger in flavor than American celery types and is used in lesser amounts. Both stems and leaves keep their flavor well when dried.

CORIANDER

CILANTRO (CHINESE PARSLEY)
Coriandrum sativum
Cantonese: *yuen sai*; **Hindi:** *dhania*; **Thai:** *pak chee*; **Vietnamese:** *ngo*

CULANTRO (SAW-LEAF HERB)
Eryngium foetidum
Thai: *pak chee farang*; **Vietnamese:** *ngo gai*

RAU RAM (VIETNAMESE CORIANDER, LAKSA LEAF)
Polygonum odoratum
Thai: *phak phai*

CORIANDER IS A UTILITARIAN herb, for all parts of the plant are used. The common names are rather confusing. Its brown seeds are called coriander. In most of the world, including Asia, its fresh leaves are known as fresh coriander, but in America, it is commonly called cilantro or Chinese parsley. No matter what you call it, this herb is among the most popular on the planet. Its aroma and rather soapy taste cause people to either relish it or dislike it intensely.

Two coriander mimics are also used in Asian cuisines: rau ram (most often known in the nursery trade by this name, but also called Vietnamese coriander), and culantro, also known in Asian markets as saw-leaf herb, which perfectly describes the shape of its long, incised leaves.

How to grow: The standard coriander is an easily grown cool-weather annual herb. It bolts to seed readily when the days start to lengthen and in warm weather. Therefore, it is best planted in the fall. In cold-winter areas, the seeds sprout the next spring after the ground thaws, and in mild-winter areas, the plants grow lush and tall. (Coriander tolerates light frosts.) In short-spring areas, early plantings are more successful than late. One guaranteed way to grow under these conditions is to treat the plant as a cut-and-come-again crop; plant seeds an inch apart and snip seedlings at ground level when they're 3 inches tall, then replant every 2 weeks until the weather gets too warm.

When possible, start coriander from seeds in place, as it withstands transplanting poorly. Plant seeds ¼ inch deep in rich, light soil and in full sun. Thin the seedlings to 6 inches and keep moist. The varieties most commonly available in nurseries, while adequate, are bred to quickly bolt and produce seeds for the world seed trade. If you choose varieties bred for leaf production instead, such as 'Long Standing' and 'Slo-Bolt,' available from mail-order seed companies, you'll harvest leaves for a longer time. Fertilize if plants get pale. Except for slugs, coriander has few pests and diseases.

Harvest sprigs once plants are 6 inches tall. When the roots are needed

Rau Ram, Vietnamese coriander *(above)*; 'Slo-Bolt' coriander *(below)*

Coriander root

easy to control. It tolerates no frost and, in cold-winter zones, is grown as an annual.

Culantro is available from specialty nurseries as seeds or plants and is an excellent cilantro substitute. It is treated as a short-lived perennial in warm-climate zones. Below Zone 9, culantro is grown as an annual. Sow seeds indoors in early winter and set seedlings out when the soil has warmed. (Seeds are slow to germinate). Grow culantro in moderately fertile, fast-draining, moist soil in full sun. In warm climates, grow it in filtered sun. It may also be grown in containers and wintered over inside. Culantro grows to 2 feet tall with a rosette of sharply toothed oblong basal leaves (growing from the crown at the base of the plant) about 4 inches long and 1 inch wide. Flowering stems grow to about 18 inches. Keep flowering stems cut back in order for a continual harvest of the basal leaves. Control slugs and snails.

Varieties

When choosing coriander (cilantro) varieties for leaf production, chose those designated as slow-bolting, available from Shepherds, Nichols, and Johnny's. See the specialty herb catalogs listed in the Resources section for culantro and Vietnamese coriander.

How to prepare: Coriander leaves are used fresh, as the flavor fades quickly when they are cooked. Generally, they are chopped and sprinkled on a dish or mixed in after cooking to give a distinct flavor. In many Asian dishes, coriander is among the most important flavorings. There is no successful way to preserve the flavor of coriander, as it fades quickly once the essential oils are exposed to air. Culantro, on the other hand, retains good flavor and color when dried, but for the best flavor it still needs to be added at the end of cooking. Culantro is most often used in dishes with beef.

Coriander seeds are used to season curries and rice dishes. The seeds are more flavorful if you toast them in a dry frying pan for a few minutes before grinding them in a spice grinder.

Coriander roots are a favored seasoning in Thai cookery. The roots are pounded together with garlic as a savory mixture in curries, particularly in red and green curry pastes (see recipe, page 86.) In recipes that call for coriander root, you can substitute coriander stems.

Rau ram is used fresh in soups, green and chicken salads, and as a fresh garnish. See the recipe for salad rolls on page 78 and for Henry's salad on page 77. In Singapore and Malaysia, the Chinese population adds rau ram to a spicy noodle dish. Rau ram is generally used fresh, for it is quite odiferous when cooked. For this reason, it is best added just before serving it in hot foods and soups.

for a recipe, harvest whole, vigorous plants using a spading fork. (Plants that have started to bolt are not suitable, as they are fibrous.) Before digging them up, loosen the soil well around the roots so they won't break.

The coriander mimics, rau ram and culantro, are tender perennials available from a few specialty herb nurseries. Rau ram is offered in plant form from herb specialists but will root in water from bunches available in Asian markets. Rau ram is a spreading plant about 1 1/2 feet tall, grown in filtered sun. It likes fertile, moist soil. It is considered invasive in areas where it thrives, but its shallow roots makes it

CORN, BABY

Zea mays

GROWING BABY CORN IS A FUN project to do with kids and the resulting cobs are sweet and crunchy, not tinny tasting like the canned ones.

How to grow: Baby corn is a different experience than sweet corn but equally rewarding. Because ears full of kernels are not the goal, plants can be crowded together and pollination and corn borers are not an issue.

All corn plants require summer heat and full sun and are best planted from seeds sown directly into the garden in organic, fertile soil. Choose from the varieties listed below. Plant seeds 1 inch deep and 3 inches apart. Thin to 6 inches. Side dress with a high-nitrogen fertilizer when plants are about 6 inches tall. Mulch with an organic mulch to control weeds and conserve moisture. Birds steal the seeds out of the ground, so cover the beds. Fertilize again when about 2 feet tall. Water regularly. Keep an eye on your plants, as baby corn is ready early in the season. The object is to harvest the cobs when they are young and tender, before they start to develop, usually within 4 days of the appearance of silks.

Varieties

Choose varieties that tend to produce multiple shoots per plant, as they give more ears.

'Baby Corn': about 65 days for immature ears; a variety especially culti-

vated for baby corn, not sweet corn; offered by Nichols Garden Nursery and Evergreen Y. H. Enterprises.

'Japanese Hulless': 100 days to popcorn, much less for baby corn, plants short, to 5 feet

'Jubilee': 85 days to mature corn; a midseason hybrid; if allowed to mature, produces sweet yellow kernels

How to prepare: Remove the husks and silks and trim the stem. Fresh baby corn needs a few more minutes of cooking then the conventional canned product.

Baby corn is most associated with China and, to a lesser degree, Japan. Sometimes it is added to sweet-and-sour recipes and stir-fries; in parts of China, it is braised in a broth with whole baby bak choy and mushrooms and glazed. It is also used as a garnish for fancy presentations, sometimes with baby pac choi and a gravy.

Close-up of baby corn *(above)*; Corn plant *(below)*

'Suyo Cross' cucumber

CUCUMBERS

Cucumis sativus
Chinese: *huang-kwa*; **Hindi:** *khira*;
Japanese: *kyuuri*; **Thai:** *taeng-kwa*

CUCUMBERS ARE ENJOYED IN
much of Asia, especially as pickles.

How to grow: Cucumbers are
warm-season annuals and tolerate no
frost. They need full sun, rich, humus-
filled soil, and ample water during the
growing season. Work bone and blood
meal into the soil before planting.
When soil and weather are warm,
plant the seeds about 1 inch deep and 6
inches apart. Thin later to 2 feet apart.
Put a trellis in place at the time of
planting. Succession planting in long-
summer areas provides cucumbers into
the fall. If plants are pale, apply fish
emulsion.

Young cucumber plants are susceptible to cutworms, snails, and striped
and spotted cucumber beetles. The
adult beetles can destroy young cucumber vines and carry diseases. Floating
row covers keep beetles away but need
to be removed when the plants flower
so bees can pollinate the flowers.

Powdery mildew is a common
problem, particularly late in the season. More serious diseases affect
cucumbers as well—mosaic virus,
scab, and anthracnose. Scab attacks the
fruits and is characterized by dry,
corky patches with a velvety olive
green growth. Anthracnose shows up
as moldy fruit and brown patches on
the leaves. Pull up affected plants, as
no cure is known for any of these conditions. When possible, plant resistant
varieties and rotate your crops.

Harvest cucumbers when they are
young and firm but filled out. Harvest
regularly or plants stop production.

Varieties

The Japanese have developed many of
today's hybrid sweet cucumbers; these
are carried by most seed companies
and often classified as "burpless."

'**Japanese Long Pickling**': 60 days; dark
green, crisp fruits to 1 foot
'**Orient Express**': 60 days; hybrid; slim,
dark green fruits; disease tolerant
'**Suyo Cross**': 61 days; hybrid with
northern China origins; large vines;
fruits ribbed, dark green to 1 foot;
disease resistant
'**Sweet Success**': 58 days; hybrid; foot-
long fruits with sweet flavor; good
disease resistance; can be grown
outside or in greenhouse

How to prepare: Cucumbers are
pickled in most of Asia and used as a
condiment. Asian cooks often sprinkle
sliced cucumbers with salt to draw out
some of the liquid before using them
in a dish. In Thailand, cucumbers are
grated with onions and dressed with
chiles, lemon juice, and fish sauce for a
salad. In India, cucumbers are considered healthful and are popular when
grated and combined with yogurt and
mint, as a salad, and as a cooked vegetable. In Sri Lanka, cucumbers are
combined with coconut milk and
chiles to accompany a curry; in Korea,
cucumber slices are sometimes stir-
fried with beef. Japanese cooks make a
soup with chicken, ginger, and cucumber wedges.

DAIKON

Raphanus sativus

Cantonese: *lo bok*; **Mandarin:** *lao bo*; **Japanese:** *daikon*; **Hindi:** *muli*

TWO TYPES OF RADISHES ARE used in Asia: the small spring European-style radishes and the very large radishes generally called Chinese radishes or by their Japanese name, daikon. The large Asian radishes are the subject here. They vary in size and shape from round globes about 6 inches in diameter to long roots of up to 2 feet. Japanese daikons are usually white, while the Chinese radishes may be white, red, or green.

Asian radishes are juicy and flavorful, ranging in taste from mild and sweet Chinese to the strong and pungent. Radish roots are served either raw or cooked. With some varieties, the leaves, seed pods, and seeds are also used. Certain varieties store well and are used as a winter staple. Varieties of strong-flavored Korean radishes are used in kim chee. High-quality daikons are fine-textured, nonfibrous radishes with juicy flesh.

Radish seeds are easily sprouted, producing highly nutritious seedlings.

How to grow: Most varieties of Asian radishes are planted in fall and mature in cool weather, but a few can be planted in the spring. Sow radish seeds directly in the garden. Plant seeds ½ inch deep; thin to 4 inches apart for smaller varieties and up to 16 inches apart for the largest. They can be planted in rows or wide beds. The soil should be light and well drained, with a generous amount of compost. Radishes are light feeders, however, so they need little fertilizer. Keep radishes consistently moist to avoid cracking and too hot a taste, though you should take care not to overwater. Keep beds weeded.

In some areas of the country, radishes are bothered by root maggots that are best controlled by rotating crops. Radishes belong to the same family as cabbages and other brassicas, so they should not follow each other. Flea beetles can also be a problem. Alternaria, clubroot, and certain viruses are potential diseases. When possible, purchase resistant varieties.

'Mino Early' and 'Red Meat' radishes

[How to Sprout Peas and Daikon]

You can sprout daikon and peas in a jar to produce curly white sprouts in the same way you do mung and soybeans are sprouted (see page 25). Or, for tastier sprouts, you can produce little green plants in a shallow container such as a paper milk carton, one side removed, laid horizontally. For drainage, punch 6 or 8 holes in the bottom. Add an inch or so of damp sand, sprinkle a few tablespoons of untreated daikon or pea seeds over it, and add a thin layer of sand on top. Water the seeds and put the container on a tray to catch the drips, then put the container in a dark closet. Keep the seeds moist but not wet. They will germinate in 3 to 5 days and grow into white, thin seedlings. When they are about 2 inches tall, bring them out into a well-lit but not sunny area to turn green. In a day or so, the young plants will be green, have a few leaves, and be ready for harvesting. To harvest, cut across the plants above the soil line with scissors.

Generally speaking, these large, long-season radishes can be harvested at any stage. After reaching maturity, they can be left in the ground for 1 to 2 months but may become tough if left much longer. They keep well if stored in a cool place. In Japan, they are sometimes left in the garden, covered with snow. For radish leaves, harvest the tender young leaves of varieties being grown for roots, or grow special varieties bred just for the leaves and harvest at any stage as needed.

Varieties

'Mino Early': 40 days; long white roots to 24 inches; crisp, mild; Japanese type; vigorous plants for spring and fall

'Misato Green': 60 days; long roots; Chinese radish with high-quality green, juicy, sweet flesh

'Misato Rose': 60 days; rose-colored flesh, light green and white skin; turnip-shaped roots about 4 inches across; tender and sweet; used fresh and pickled; not for spring planting

'Miyashige': 60 days; a white-fleshed, green-necked fall radish with crisp flesh; popular for pickling

'Shinrimei' ('Red Meat'): Chinese "beauty heart" radish with white skin, green shoulders, and red flesh; good raw or cooked

How to prepare: Throughout Asia, the young, tender green tops of Asian radishes are braised or added to soups, and radish roots are washed, scraped, and cut up or grated for addition to soups and other dishes.

The Chinese use cooked radishes in many ways but rarely use the root raw. They often stir-fry radishes after salting and draining them. The stir-fries include pork, shrimp, or shellfish. Also, radishes are made into hearty winter soups and stews. Chinese sauces sometimes contain grated radishes.

According to Elizabeth Andoh, author of Japanese cookbooks, in Japan, daikon is "the all-impressive, all-purpose, absolutely everything kind of vegetable. When it's in season, it would be hard to find anybody in Japan who hadn't eaten a daikon within three days." Daikon is usually finely grated and often mixed with soy sauce to make a dipping sauce served with tempura and other dishes. Chunks of daikon can be steamed and sauced with miso. A traditional New Year dish is julienned strips of daikon, carrots, and dried apricots served with a sweet-and-sour sauce. Daikons are pickled in rice vinegar or rice wine and soy sauce or prepared as salt pickles, which are used as an accompaniment to the meal or added to dishes as a flavoring. They are also braised or used in fish stew, soups, and salads.

EGGPLANTS

Solanum melongena

Chinese: *ngai gwa*; **India:** *brinjal*;
Japanese: *nasubi*; **Thai:** *makhua terung*

THE MOST COMMON EGGPLANT
in Asia is long, thin, and purple.

How to grow: Eggplants are tender
perennials, usually grown as annuals.
Eggplants tolerate no cold; start seeds
indoors 6 weeks before the average
date of your last frost. The seeds germinate best at 80°F. Plant the seeds ¼
inch deep, in flats or peat pots. When
all danger of frost is past and the soil is
warm, mulch with organic matter and
transplant the seedlings into the garden 2 feet apart; water well. Grow
eggplants in full sun in rich, well-
drained, fertile garden loam. Work a
balanced organic fertilizer for vegetables into the soil before planting at the
rate recommended on the package.
Stake the plants to prevent them from
falling over with a heavy harvest. To
increase yield and to keep the plants
healthy, feed them with fish emulsion
twice during the summer. If you are
growing eggplants in a cool climate,
cover the soil with black or red plastic
to retain heat. Eggplants need moderate watering and should never be
allowed to dry out.

Flea beetles, spider mites, and
whiteflies can be a problem. Spider
mites can be a nuisance in warm, dry
weather. Nematodes are sometimes a
problem in the South. Verticillium wilt
and phomopsis blight are common disease problems in humid climates.

Eggplant is ready to harvest when it
is full colored but has not yet begun to
lose any of its sheen. Press down on the
eggplant with your finger; if the flesh
presses in and bounces back, it is ripe.

Varieties

'Asian Bride': 70 days; white skins
streaked with lavender; 6 inches
long, 1 ½ inches in diameter

'Bharta': 60 days to flower; East Indian
variety; large, round purple-black
fruits with few seeds; productive

'Green Tiger': 75 days; Thai variety
with pale green fruits with dark
green stripes; 1 to 2 inches round;
plants 3 feet tall, productive

'Harabegan': 60 days to flowering;
elongated (to 10 inches), shiny green
fruits with few seeds; East Indian
variety

'Ichiban Hybrid': 61 days; long, slender, high-quality purple fruits;
high-yielding plants

'Ping Tung': 75 days; slender, lavender
to purple fruits to 18 inches long;
prolific; heat and humidity tolerant;
traditional Taiwanese variety

How to prepare: The standard
Asian eggplants have tender skin and
little bitterness, and therefore needn't
be peeled or salted. Chinese cooking
methods for eggplants include braising
and frying. In Shantung, cooked eggplant is served cold with a sesame
sauce and, in Szechwan, eggplants are
fried and served in a spicy sauce. In
Japan, eggplant is used in tempura,
baked and served with a variety of
sauces, including a dipping sauce of
grated ginger and soy sauce, braised in

Japanese eggplant

sesame and bean sauce, and pickled. In
Thailand, eggplants are usually used in
sweet-and-sour dishes or in curries. In
India, eggplants are often stuffed and
cooked in a savory sauce or baked and
the flesh mixed with spices (see recipe,
page 85).

GARLIC

Allium sativum

Cantonese: *suen tau/tao*; **Mandarin:** *suan*; **Japanese:** *nin-niku*

GARLIC IS POPULAR IN ALL OF Asia, with two notable exceptions. The Japanese avoid it because of its lingering odor and the Brahmans in India do because they believe it stirs the baser passions. On the other hand, in much of Asia, people value its medicinal properties.

How to grow: Garlic plants are grown from cloves that can be purchased as heads in the nurseries. Although easily grown, garlic performs best in mild, dry climates. It's best planted in the fall or early spring. Garlic prefers full sun and a well-drained, loose soil rich in organic matter and phosphorus.

Divide the heads into individual cloves and plant them about 1 1/2 inches deep and 4 inches apart. In cold-winter areas, mulch with straw to protect fall-started plants. Consistent moisture is needed for the first 4 months. Fertilize in early spring, when the leaves are growing, with an organic source of nitrogen. Plants with healthy, leafy growth produce the best bulbs. Decrease your watering once the leaves fill out.

In Asia, whole young garlic plants are sometimes harvested, as are the flowering stalks. Garlic greens are also sometimes lightly harvested and used in cooking as you would scallions, providing the plants are not depleted.

Young garlic plants

Garlic is ready for harvest when the plant tops turn brown (the ideal moment is when about half of the leaves are still green). Dig the heads and allow them to dry on a screen in the shade, protected from sunburn. To prevent rotting and to allow braiding, retain several inches of dried stalk on each head. Store garlic in a cool, dry area with good air circulation.

Varieties

'Georgian Crystal': large white bulbs; very mild flavor, good raw; stores well

'Gilroy California Late': good flavor, juicy cloves, long keeping; ideal for braiding

'German Extra-Hardy': very winter-hardy, good for northern gardens, good flavor, keeps well

'Romanian Red': cloves streaked with red; hot and pungent; stores very well

How to prepare: In China, garlic cloves are used in almost all meat, poultry, and vegetable stir-fries; in stews, and in marinades for grilling. In northern China, whole young garlic plants are sometimes stir-fried with smoked pork, and a traditional dish of steamed prawns calls for great amounts of minced garlic. Garlic is a favorite in Korea where, along with chiles, it is an integral to the national dish, kim chee, and popular in many cooked dishes. In India and Southeast Asia, garlic is often included in curries of all sorts. In fact, author Charmaine Solomon describes a dish of southern India where whole garlic is treated as a vegetable and cooked in a curry sauce. In addition, whole garlic cloves are pickled and enjoyed in most of Asia.

GARLIC CHIVES
(CHINESE CHIVES)

Allium tuberosum
Cantonese: *gau tsoi*; **Japanese:** *nira*;
Mandarin: *jiu cai*; **Thai:** *kui chaai*;
Vietnamese: *he*

CHINESE LEEK
(CHINESE LEEK FLOWER)

Allium ramosum (A. odorum)
Cantonese: *gau choi fa*

GARLIC CHIVES ARE A FAIRLY
common herb in the West. In contrast,
Chinese leek is rarely available and is a
variety grown primarily for its young,
tender flower stems and buds. Both of
these Asian alliums are related to common chives (*A. schoenoprasum*) and
have an onion-garlic flavor, narrow,
flat leaves to 2 feet tall, and flat sprays
of white, star-shaped flowers. Both are
perennial plants hardy to USDA Zone
3 and native to Asia.

How to grow: These alliums are
best planted in spring. They need at
least 6 hours of sun daily and average
to rich, well-drained, moist soil.
Seedlings grow slowly and, in short climates, usually take the entire season to
mature from seeds, so they are not harvested the first year.

Once established, garlic chives
bloom but once, in early fall. Chinese
leeks, on the other hand, bloom at least
twice throughout the spring and summer and produce multiple stems with

Chinese chives, blanched

fat flower buds. These alliums grow
best and are most tender and succulent
if fertilized in spring and later, too, if
the leaves turn pale. In rainy areas,
supplemental water is seldom needed,
and pests (except for occasional black
aphids) and diseases are few.

Harvest the leaves a few at a time or
cut the entire plant down to the crown
when the leaves are tender and lush. If
you have not harvested them heavily,
cut them back after they flower to tidy
and renew the plants. Remove the seed
heads on garlic chives, as they reseed
readily and can become a nuisance.
Divide all plants every 3 or 4 years.

In Asia, mature chive plants are
sometimes blanched in the garden to
produce yellow, tender leaves and
stalks. This is done by completely
excluding light. Plants at least a year
old are first cut to the ground and a
solid container 10 or so inches deep is
inverted over the crowns to exclude the
light. Within 10 days to 3 weeks, long,

pale leaves are ready for harvest. To
prevent weakening the plant, blanching is usually done but once a year.

Varieties

Garlic chives can be obtained as divisions, transplants, and seeds. Chinese
leeks are seldom available, and then
only from seeds. Seeds of both are
available from Evergreen Y. H.
Enterprises.

How to prepare: These Asian alliums have a strong taste, more like garlic than onion, and tend to get stringy
and tasteless when overcooked. The
green leaves of Chinese chives are
often cut in sections 1 or 2 inches long
and used in stir-fries with meat and
oyster sauce, pork, chicken, and bean
curd; in soups; simmered in broth; and
braised and served alone as a vegetable.
In much of northern China, chopped
chives are used in steamed and fried
breads and in dumplings. Chinese leek
flower stems and buds are often used
in the same manner. Prepare them as
you would asparagus, by removing any
tough lower parts of the stem.

Yellow chives are the blanched
leaves of garlic chives. Blanching renders them softer, with a sweet and mellow onion flavor. They require only
brief cooking and are usually added to
a dish at the last minute. They are stir-fried with noodles, pork, and poultry
as well as used in soups and steamed
dishes. See the pea shoots with crab
sauce recipe on page 71.

In Japan, chive leaves are cut in
lengths and added to soups and sukiyaki or used whole as a garnish.

GINGER
(TRUE GINGER)

Zingiber officinale
Chinese: *saa jiang*

MIOGA GINGER

Z. mioga
Hindi: *chandramala;* **Thai:** *proh hom*

TRUE GINGER CAN GROW TO 4 feet. The leaves are narrow and a light, bright green. Both the shoots and rhizomes are edible. Mioga ginger is grown for its flower buds and leaves. The rhizomes are not edible.

How to grow: Gingers are tender, deciduous perennials needing long, warm, humid summers. They are worth trying in cooler or drier climates but tend to be temperamental and should be considered an experiment. Gingers prefer bright light to hot sun, so plant in a warm, fairly shady spot. They also need rich, moist soil with good drainage, as they will rot in cold, wet soil. Keep well watered. In tropical regions, true ginger is planted in early spring and the rhizomes harvested 9 months later, in late fall. In cold-winter areas, start ginger in the house, planting outside when the weather warms up. Ginger can also be grown as a houseplant. Move up to larger pots as it grows.

True ginger can be harvested after 5 months when it has plenty of full-grown leaves, but for the biggest harvest, wait for 8 or 9 months. If the weather becomes too cold, either harvest the rhizomes or bring the entire

Ginger sprouts *(above)*; ginger plant *(center)*; and Mioga ginger flower buds, ready for harvest *(below)*

plant into the house for the fall and let it grow in a well-lit room until fully mature. When harvesting, save a rhizome to replant, thus maintaining your own source of this delightful flavoring.

Mioga ginger is a Japanese ginger that is more tolerant of colder climates. The flowers and leaves are harvested while young. The leaves are usually blanched before harvesting by covering so that light cannot reach them. The flowers buds are harvested just before they emerge from the soil and before they are open by breaking them off the parent rhizome.

Varieties
Fresh rhizomes of true ginger, called ginger root, are available at produce stands or in Asian markets. Choose rhizomes that show good growth buds (like eyes on a potato). True ginger is also offered by Richters Herbs and The Banana Tree. Mioga ginger is rare but sometimes available from nurseries that cater to a Japanese clientele. I purchased mine from a vendor at my local farmers' market.

How to prepare: Mature ginger is stronger in flavor than freshly dug, thin-skinned young ginger. Ginger root is peeled and sliced in a dish then removed, or very finely minced and left in the cooked dish. Ginger is used in all of Asia to add a lovely spicy flavor to soups, stews, dressings, and stir-fries. See the many stir-fries in the recipe section to get a feel for how to use ginger. Mioga ginger flowers and leaves are used for flavoring in stir-fries (see recipe, page 68) and soups.

LEMON GRASS
(CITRONELLA GRASS)

Cymbopogon citratus
Hindi: *herva chaha;* **Indonesian:** *sereh;*
Thai: *ta krai;* **Vietnamese:** *xa*

A CITRUS-SCENTED GRASS-FAMILY
herb, lemon grass is prized in
Southeast Asia. This tropical perennial
is a large, clump-forming herb that
grows to 3 feet in temperate climates.
The lemon-scented oils are in the
stems.

How to grow: Lemon grass can be
grown outdoors in climates where the
temperature stays above the mid-twen-
ties and in containers in cold climates,
if brought inside in winter. Plant divisions in good, fast-draining soil in partial shade. Fertilize the plants a few
times during the growing season and
keep the soil moist. Lemon grass has
few disease and pest problems.

Lemon grass plant *(above),* and how to mince
(below)

Varieties

Purchase divisions from specialty seed
companies. If a few roots are attached,
sometimes a stalk from the market will
root.

How to prepare: Harvest the white
leafstalks by cutting them at the base of
the plant once it's established. Use
them to flavor chicken stock-based
soups, with or without coconut milk,
and fish stock-based soups. Lemon
grass is also used in salad dressings and
to make a fragrant cup of tea (see
recipe, page 65). Depending on the

recipe, the stalks are cut into 2-inch
lengths, sliced thinly crosswise, or
coarsely chopped. Usually the stalks
are removed from a dish before serving, but they are also minced and
added to stir-fries and curries or
pounded together with other herbs to
form a paste for adding to a dish (see
the Thai curry recipe on page 88). To
preserve lemon grass, either dry it or
freeze the fleshy stalks.

LIME LEAF
(KAFFIR LIME,
FRAGRANT LIME)

Citrus hystrix
Indonesian: *jeruk perut;* **Thai:** *bai
magrood;* **Vietnamese:** *la chanh*

LIME LEAF IS AN EVERGREEN
citrus—a small tree with rounded
leaves indented on either side, and
with knobby fruit. Its fragrant leaves
and thick green rind are used in cooking. The juice from the fruit is sour
and seldom utilized.

How to grow: Lime leaf is grown
outside where there is no frost; in other
regions, grow it in containers and
bring it indoors in winter. Plant the
tree in a large pot in fast-draining soil.
Maintain a regular watering schedule;
through the summer, fertilize once a
month with citrus fertilizer.

Lime leaf plant

Lime leaf with fruit

Outside, grow lime leaf in well-drained organic soil. Add a citrus fertilizer according to the directions on the package. Grow lime leaf in full sun. Beginning in the spring, feed with citrus fertilizer, tapering off in late summer to discourage new growth susceptible to frost.

Varieties

Pacific Tree Farms ships lime leaf.

How to prepare: Kaffir lime leaves may be harvested when the tree is established and its leaves are at least 3 inches long. The fragrant leaves function in cooking like bay leaves, slowly releasing their citrus flavor in long-simmered dishes, soups, and curries. They are excellent in fish dishes and can be minced and ground to a paste with other herbs and spices such as coriander root, lemon grass, and garlic to add to curries (see recipe, page 88), chicken, and other meat dishes. The fresh leaves may be wrapped tightly in plastic wrap and frozen for future use. Finely shredded, the rind may be sprinkled over salads and added to curries during the last few moments of cooking.

LUFFA, ANGLED
(CHINESE OKRA, RIDGED SKIN LUFFA)

Luffa acutangula
Hindi: *kali tori;* **Mandarin:** *si gua;*
Cantonese: *sze kwa*

LUFFA, SMOOTH
(SPONGE GOURD)

L. cylindrica
Hindi: *ghiya tori;* **Mandarin:** *si gua;*
Cantonese: *see kwa;* **Japanese:** *hechima*

THE TWO TYPES OF LUFFA ARE both annual vining plants in the cucumber family. Their fruits, associated with Chinese cooking, are eaten as a vegetable when young. *Luffa acutangula* has long, narrow fruits with ridged skin and large, fragrant yellow flowers. *L. cylindrica* has more cylindrical fruits with smoother skin.

How to grow: The cultivation of both luffas is the same. They need a long, warm growing season. Grow and maintain them as you would cucumbers (see the entry for Cucumbers). Harvest the fruits when they are still immature and about 6 inches long.

Varieties

Many catalogs list luffa simply under the common names. While unstated in the catalog, some varieties are short-day plants and don't flower in northern latitudes.

'Edible Ace': smooth, green fruits; 8 to 15 inches long, 3 inches across; use the immature fruits for a vegetable; good matured for bath sponges

Chinese Okra: 90 days; the immature flesh is very tender and sweet; no peeling necessary

How to prepare: Luffa fruits are edible only when immature. Cook them much as you would zucchini. The flower buds, young shoots, and young leaves are edible and may be added to stir-fries. The whole fruits can be stuffed with ground pork and braised. A traditional Chinese soup is made with pork or chicken broth and bean curd cubes. Just before serving the soup, thinly sliced luffa is added and briefly cooked.

Do not eat the mature fruits; they are extremely bitter and are a strong laxative.

Luffa sponge gourd (*top*) and luff flower*above*)

MITSUBA

(JAPANESE PARSLEY; TREFOIL)

Cryptotaenia japonica
Cantonese: *san ip;* **Mandarin:** *san ye qin*

THE WORD *MITSUBA* MEANS "three leaves" in Japanese. Mitsuba looks and tastes a bit like Italian parsley, with dark green, trifoliate leaves and long, pale stems. In Japanese cuisine, every part of the herb is used—leaves, leaf-stalks, roots, and seeds.

How to grow: Mitsuba grows to 3 feet tall and is usually treated as an annual, although it's a perennial. Start mitsuba from seed, sow 1/4 inch deep, and thin to 1 foot apart. Mitsuba is a woodland plant. Grow it in moist soil in partial shade and keep plants moist.

Harvest a few leaves once the plant is established and the young stems as you need them once they are a foot tall. When the older stems become tough, they can be used in longer-cooking dishes. Let a few plants go to seed for the next year's planting.

In Japan, mitsuba is sometimes garden blanched in the same manner as celery.

Varieties

Unnamed mitsuba is carried by Kitazawa Seed Company and Evergreen Y. H. Enterprises.

How to prepare: Mitsuba leaves and stems are boiled for a minute or two and eaten as a green, raw in salads, pickled in vinegar, fried in tempura batter, added to soups, including

Mitsuba

eggdrop soup, and used for flavoring and as a garnish. When used in soups or as a garnish, the leaves and stems are generally chopped and added in the last minute of cooking.

According to herb maven Holly Shimizu, often, on important occasions—a wedding or the finalizing of a business contract—several stalks of mitsuba are tied together in a knot and added to a dish for decoration. In Japan, the knot is considered an auspicious symbol.

Mizuna

MIBUNA

(MIBU GREENS)

Brassica spp.

MIZUNA

(POT-HERB MUSTARD)

B. rapa var. *japonica*
Mandarin: *shui cai;* **Japanese:** *kyona, mizuna*

MUSTARD

HEADED (WRAPPED HEART)

Brassica juncea
Mandarin: *bao xin da jie cai;* **Cantonese:** *yeh choi;* **Japanese:** *kekkyu takana*

MUSTARD

JAPANESE RED

Brassica juncea var. *rugosa*

IN GENERAL, ASIAN MUSTARDS are mild to pungent loose-leafed vegetables that grow from one to several feet in height. Most prefer cool growing conditions. Headed mustards form heads of pale green, thin-textured leaves that curl inward and are grown mainly for pickling. Japanese red mustards have bronze red leaves that are quite peppery. Mizuna is a strikingly beautiful cut-leafed vegetable that is popular in Japan. Mibuna is a mild-flavored Japanese green with a pleasant mustardy taste. Mibuna plants, which can grow up to 2 feet, have multiple stems with slender, smooth leaves at the end of each.

'Giant Red Mustard' cut-and-come-again *(above)*; 'Giant Red Mustard' with mizuna in bloom in back; 'Osaka Purple' with peas; Shirona mustard showing slug and army worm damage

How to grow: Mustards are fast-growing cool-season crops. They do best in a fertile organic soil with good drainage. Plant seeds in full sun, 1/4 inch deep and 3 inches apart, in early spring or fall. Thin to 1 foot apart if growing to maturity. Alternately, broadcast the seeds of Japanese mustard or mizuna and grow as baby greens in a cut-and-come-again method by themselves or mixed. For mature heads of headed mustard, sow in midsummer or early fall for fall or early winter harvest.

Mustards need sufficient moisture while growing or they may become too spicy to eat. Mustards are relatively disease free, although, as members of the cabbage family, they are occasionally plagued by pests that bother that group (see the entry for Chinese Cabbage).

Harvest a few leaves at a time as they are needed. For Japanese red mustard, the younger the leaf, the milder. Mizuna tends to tolerate both heat and cold, so it can be harvested over a long time. Harvest headed mustards mature heads as you would cabbage.

Varieties

Pickling Mustards

'Nan-fong': Chinese mustard; heat tolerant; can be planted spring through fall; large leaves and thick stems

'Green-in-the-Snow': very hardy; vigorous

Japanese Red Mustard

'Osaka Purple': 40 days; milder and more compact than 'Giant Red'; leaves purple with white veins; great for baby greens

'Red Giant Mustard': 45 days; deep purple red savoyed leaves; tangy leaves; great for baby greens

Mibuna and Mizuna

Named varieties of mibuna and mizuna may not be listed. Mizuna is quick-growing and days to maturity start at 45 days.

'Green Spray': 40 days; early; a robust hybrid mibuna with crunchy texture and mild flavor; winter hardy

'Tokyo Beau': a slow-bolting, vigorous hybrid mizuna; large plants with large leaves

How to prepare: In China, the strong-flavored mustards are often combined with ginger and used in soups, blanched and served with oil or oyster sauce, or stir-fried with meat and bean sauce. In Japan, the mustards are sometimes braised, used as salt pickles, or cooked in soups and stir-fries. Some mustards are mainly grown for pickling (see recipe, on page 65), though they are also eaten fresh. Pickled and cut, they add a real flavor boost to soups and stir-fries (see recipe, page 69).

PAC CHOI

Brassica rapa var. *chinensis*
Mandarin: *bai cai;* **Japanese:** *chingensai*

TATSOI

(ROSETTE PAK CHOI, FLAT CABBAGE)

B. rapa var. *rosularis*
Mandarin: *wu ta cai;* **Cantonese:** *tai koo choi;* **Japanese:** *tatsoi*

PAC CHOI IS A DELIGHTFUL non-heading leafy green with swordlike, spoonlike, or open and flat leaves. Choice varieties include a compact, vase-shaped plant with misty green stalks, sometimes referred to as Shanghai pac choi, and tatsoi, an attractive plant with deep green leaves arranged in a flat rosette.

How to grow: Pac choi is grown as mustard (see previous page). It tends to get stringy in hot weather; some varieties, however, are heat tolerant. Tatsoi is quite cold tolerant. Give plants a half-strength feeding of fish emulsion when planting, a supplemental feeding about a month after planting, and again at the beginning of head development. 'Joi Choi' and the Shanghai pac choi can be grown as cut-and-come-again baby greens. See "The Pleasures of a Stir-fry Garden" on page 11 for more information.

Harvest shoots, individual leaves, or the whole plant, or use the cut-and-come-again method with the tall pac choi. As a rule, the younger the plant,

Clockwise from above left: Tatsoi; Pack choi 'Joi Choi,' pack choi as cut and come again; 'Mei Qing' pac choi

the tenderer. The flowering types of pac choi are grown for their flower buds and stalks, so harvest them when the buds form.

Varieties

Green-Leafed, White-Stemmed Pac Choi

'Joi Choi': 45 days; hybrid; vigorous; productive white stalks with deep green leaves

Green-Stemmed Pac Choi

'Chinese Pac Choi': 65 days; fast-growing, cold-resistant, compact plant; glossy leaves

'Mei Qing Choi': 45 days; a baby Shanghai pac choi; bolt resistant; uniform

'Shanghai Pak Choi': 50 days; heat tolerant, can be grown spring to fall in many climates

Tatsoi (Tah Tsai): 45 days; deep green, spoon-shaped leaves form a tight rosette

How to prepare: In China, pac choi is most commonly used in stir-fries and soups (see recipe, page 66) with meat and seasonings, and braised and served with a sauce. In Canton, it is served with roast pork or a black bean sauce. Often, whole baby pac choi are blanched and arranged on a platter with cooked mushrooms or seafood and glazed with a flavorful sauce.

PEAS

EDIBLE-PODDED (SNOW PEAS)

Pisum sativum var. *macrocarpon*

Chinese: *ho lan tau;* **Japanese:** *saya endo*

PEA SPROUTS

P. sativum

Mandarin: *dou miao;* **Cantonese:** *dau miu;* **Japanese:** *tobyo*

PEA SHOOTS AND LEAVES

P. sativum

THE POPULAR PEAS OF THE Orient are the edible-podded ones. Pea sprouts and shoots are also considered delicacies.

How to grow: Pea plants are either short bushes or long climbing vines that require well-drained organic soil, full sun, and cool weather. They tolerate some frost but do poorly in hot weather. Seeds should be planted 1 inch deep and 4 inches apart. Most varieties need some form of support, which should be placed in the ground at planting time. Peas need only a light fertilizing at midseason but profit from regular and deep watering. If growing just for pea shoots, pinch back the growing points when the plants are about 4 inches high to encourage the plant to be bushier and produce more shoots.

Pea seedlings are ambrosia to slugs, snails, and birds, and thrips and

'Sopporo Express' snow peas; 'Oregon Giant' snow peas

mildew are problems under some conditions.

Pick snow peas when the pods are still soft and pliable and the seeds inside are still small. For pea leaves and shoots, snip off the top of the shoots, including the top few leaves and tendrils, starting when the plants are about a foot high.

How to grow sprouts: See the information on growing daikon and pea shoots on page 40.

Varieties

Snow Peas

'Dwarf Gray Sugar': bush, to about 2 feet; very productive with tender and delicious pods; a good variety to use for pea shoots

'Oregon Giant': 70 days; bush, to 3 feet; large, sweet, and succulent pods; plants are resistant to powdery mildew and fusarium wilt

'Sopporo Express': 40 days; baby snow peas; purple flowers; tall vines; vigorous, hardy, available from Redwood City Seeds

Snow Pea Shoots and Leaves

While most varieties of peas can be used for pea shoots, Evergreen Y. H. Enterprises carries a snow pea variety (designated snow pea shoots) cultivated for shoots.

How to prepare: Succulent, sweet pea pods are popular in Chinese cooking. They are usually stir-fried until just cooked through, only a minute or two, and can easily be made mushy by overcooking. They go well with shrimp and poultry. In China, pea shoots are braised and served with fish balls or stir-fried and served with crab (see recipe, page 71). Pea sprouts are a luxury dish that is usually simply stir-fried with little seasoning except oil and garlic.

PEPPERS

Capsicum annuum

Cantonese: *laat jiu;* **Hindi:** *mirch;*
Japanese: *togarashi;* **Thai:** *prik chee faa;*
Vietnamese: *ot*

HOT ASIAN PEPPERS ARE MOST
associated with the cooking of
Southern Asia. A few sweet peppers
are occasionally grown as well.

How to grow: Peppers are tender
perennials, usually grown as warm-
weather annuals. Start and grow them
as you would eggplants (see page 41),
but give them less nitrogen, as too
much favors leaf growth over fruits.
Generally, peppers have fewer pest
problems than eggplants.

Once peppers get full size, you can
pick them at any color stage, but they
have more flavor after they ripen. Cut,
rather than pull, the peppers.

Varieties

Hot Peppers

'Chi-chien': very hot, medium-sized
red peppers; good fresh or dried
'Large Red Thick Cayenne': 76 days;
wrinkled, 6 inches long, 1 1/4 inches
wide; pendant fruits; pungent
'Thai Dragon Hybrid': 70 days; similar
to 'Thai Hot' but larger; tall plants
'Thai Hot': 80 days; from Thailand;
small, thin pods to 1 1/2 inches in
length; green to red; extremely hot;
grows well in warmer regions

Sweet Peppers

'Shishito': 4-inch green to red wrinkled
fruits; popular in Japan

How to prepare: Throughout much
of southern Asia, hot peppers yield the
spiciness characteristic of many
cuisines—Szechwan-style stir-fries and
soups, for instance, and Indian and
Thai curries, Korean kim chee, Thai
satay, and Vietnamese dipping sauces.
Hot peppers are added to a dish whole,
fresh, or dried; they may be grated or
chopped. Hot oils, made by simmering
peanut oil with hot pepper flakes, are
used to flavor stir-fries, as are pastes

Pictured in photo above: 'Thai Hot' *(above);*
'Shishito' *(middle);* 'Thai Dragon' *(below)*

made from reconstituted dried peppers. The amount of hot pepper used
in a dish in Asia is enormous compared the amount that would be added
to the same dish in the West. In fact,
authentic dishes from India and
Southeast Asia take some working
up to.

Red and green perilla *(left);* 'Bronze' perilla *(right)*

PERILLA
(BEEFSTEAK PLANT)

Perilla frutescens

Japanese: *shiso* (green perilla or red
perilla, *P. frutescens* 'Atropurpurea');
Mandarin: *zi su;* **Vietnamese:** *tia to*

IN JAPAN, AROMATIC PERILLA is
popular and comes in two forms: green
and purple (red). The flat-leafed green
variety is spicier than the more crinkled purple perilla. A cultivar of perilla
with two-tone leaves—green on top
and purple underneath, sold as
'Bronze' perilla—is the perilla of
choice in Vietnam.

How to grow: Both the green and
purple varieties of perilla are large
annual plants grown in the same manner as basil (see page 23). Perilla grows
to about 3 feet and is handsome in the

garden. If seed heads are not removed,
however, perilla can self-seed and
become a nuisance.

Varieties

Red and green perilla are available as
seeds from Richters. Look for 'Bronze'
perilla in specialty herb nurseries and
in local Asian markets.

How to prepare: The young leaves
and seeds are used in different ways in
Japan. The flower stalks of the green
perilla are sometimes arranged on a
sashimi platter; the diner takes the
chopsticks and rubs the flowers off into
the dipping sauce and the flowers cling
to the fish as it is eaten. Green perilla
has a somewhat cinnamon flavor and,
in Japan, it is wrapped around sushi
and its leaves are made into a tempura.
Purple perilla leaves taste a little of
anise; Japanese cooks used them to flavor tofu, as a garnish for tempura, and

to add color to pickled ginger (see
recipe, page 64). Occasionally, they are
dried and sprinkled over rice.

Chinese cooks generally prefer purple perilla to green; they use it for flavoring seafood and in pickling. In
Vietnam, perilla leaves are wrapped
around grilled meats or served raw in
salads; in Korea, the seeds are added to
marinades or ground and added to
soups.

SESAME

Sesamum indicum
Chinese: *chih ma, zhi ma;*
Japanese: *goma*

SESAME SEEDS HAVE A distinctive, nutty flavor popular in Asian cuisine. The upright plants grow to 3 feet and have pleasant foliage and white or pink flowers.

How to grow: Sesame, a tropical plant grown as an annual, needs a long, warm growing season. Otherwise, it is fairly easy to grow. Gardeners in warm climates can start seeds in the garden after all chance of frost is past. Sow ½ inch deep and 6 inches apart. In cooler climates, sesame must be started inside. The plants do not transplant well; start in peat pots so that you do not disturb the roots when transplanting.

Harvest the seeds before the seed pods burst open.

Varieties

Sesame seeds are carried by Richters Herbs and Kitazawa Seed Company.

How to prepare: In Asia, sesame seeds are used whole or ground in dressings for steamed and blanched greens. See the recipe for Japanese-style sesame dressing for shungiku greens on page 86 and a Korean dish of bean sprouts with sesame seeds on page 84. Ground sesame seeds are popular in Japan in miso soup. In China, sesame seeds are sometimes added to stir-fries.

Sesame flowers

SHUNGIKU

CHRYSANTHEMUM GREENS; GARLAND CHRYSANTHEMUM

Chrysanthemum coronarium
Cantonese: *tung ho;* **Mandarin:** *tung hao;* **Japanese:** *shungiku, shungiku;* **Thai:** *khee kwai*

SHUNGIKU, A CLOSE RELATIVE of the garden chrysanthemum, is especially popular in Japan. An annual, shungiku is cultivated for its succulent and tangy leaves and stems, which are eaten raw or cooked. The yellow, white, or orange single petals are enjoyed as well.

How to grow: Plant shungiku in rich organic soil. These are fast-growing, cool weather plants. Sow seeds ¼ inch deep in early spring or early fall in full sun or part shade in hot climates. Fertilize with fish meal or blood meal at planting time; give another supplemental feeding about a month later. Keep the plants moist but not wet.

When the plants are 4 to 6 inches tall, harvest individual leaves or the whole plant. As a rule, the younger the plant, the milder the leaves. Leaves turn bitter in warm weather.

Varieties

Most of the recommended seed sources carry some form of shungiku greens. The days to maturity range from 40 to 80 days.

How to prepare: Shungiku leaves can be blanched in boiling water for a few seconds, which gives them a dark green color (and makes older leaves more suitable). Quickly cool the leaves in cold water after blanching, then drizzle with a dashi- or sesame-based dressing (see recipe, page 86). Stir-fry the leaves or make a traditional Cantonese soup of pork or chicken stock with vegetables and mushrooms. In Japan, the most popular uses for shungiku are in sukiyaki and other rich soups and braised dishes. Occasionally, the flower petals are sprinkled over soups and salads for a garnish. In China, the flowers are dried and used for a refreshing tea (see recipe, page 65).

SPINACH

Spinacia oleracea

MALABAR SPINACH (CEYLON SPINACH)

Basella alba (Basella rubra)

Mandarin: *luo kui;* **Cantonese:** *san choi;*
Japanese: *tsuru-murasaki*

ASIAN VARIETIES OF SPINACH, primarily bred in Japan, are similar to Western varieties but have smooth leaves.

Malabar spinach is a quick-growing, tropical climbing vine. The young leaves are used like spinach in tropical areas. Red Malabar spinach has green leaves and red stems.

How to grow: If the weather is cool and the soil is rich and filled with humus, standard spinach is easy to grow. As it is a cool-season crop, spinach bolts if the weather is too warm. As a rule, though, smooth-leafed Asian spinach varieties tolerate heat better than most. Sow seeds in early spring or fall, or in winter in mild-winter areas. Plant seeds $^1/_2$ inch deep and about 1 inch apart in full sun and in rich, well-drained soil. Keep fairly moist. Thin seedlings to 3 inches apart. Spinach has occasional problems with slugs and leaf miners, plus downy mildew under fall conditions. Harvest spinach leaves a few at a time, as needed, by pinching off; or harvest the entire plant.

Malabar spinach needs warm growing conditions. It is a tender perennial that can grow to 20 feet in tropical regions, but it is grown as an annual, reaching around 6 feet in temperate areas. Sow in spring or early summer in a fertile soil with good drainage. Give the plant plenty of moisture. Malabar spinach has few pest problems. Harvest the young leaves and tips.

Varieties

Asian-Type Spinach

'Hiyoshimaru': year-round Japanese hybrid

'Megathon': 60 days; Stokes' "best Oriental spinach"; downy mildew tolerant; sow in spring

'Tamina': 60 days; smooth, tender leaves; slow to bolt

Asian spinach varieties: 'Tamina' and 'Tyee' on left and American varieties on the right

Red Malabar spinach

'Tyee': 53 days; fairly smooth leaves; tolerates downy mildew; slow to bolt

Malabar Spinach
Evergreen Y. H. Enterprises and Nichols Garden Nursery carry Malabar spinach.

How to prepare: Numerous Asian dishes call for "any green vegetable" and spinach is perfect for these. More specifically, Chinese cooks use spinach with noodles and in stir-fries. Spinach is braised and served with a sesame dressing in Japan (see recipe, page 86), and used in tempura. In India, spinach is combined with spices and butter and puréed (see recipe, page 82.) In most of Asia, the most common use of both types of spinach is in soups. Malabar spinach has a slippery texture not unlike okra, and it is used to thicken many types of soup.

TURNIPS

Brassica rapa var. *rapifera*
Mandarin: *wujing;* **Cantonese:** *mo ching;* **Japanese:** *kabu*

ASIAN TURNIPS ARE USUALLY eaten when quite young and are enjoyed as a pickle as well as raw.

How to grow: Turnips prefer cool weather and need well-drained, loose soil. They need little fertilizing if planted in good soil. Plant turnips in place in early spring or fall. Plant the seed about $1/2$ inch deep in rows or wide beds. Turnip seeds germinate quickly. Thin to 2 inches apart for baby turnips, 4 inches apart for larger ones. Use thinnings cooked or in salads. Keep moist, or the turnips turn bitter.

Turnips mature in 1 to 2 months. Many people prefer young, tender baby turnips. These can be planted in early spring for harvest before warm weather but are sweeter when planted in late summer for harvest in the fall.

Varieties

'Nozawana': bred especially for the greens, which are used pickled and stir-fried; heat and cold resistant

'Scarlet Ball': old Asian favorite; scarlet skin with white flesh; when pickled, it turns bright scarlet

'Shogoin': 30 days greens; 60 days roots; has tender, mild greens and 6-inch roots especially good for cooking and pickling

'Tokyo Cross': 34 days; very early; high-quality white turnip with sweet flesh

How to prepare: In Asia, young turnips are enjoyed pickled, sliced and served raw with a dressing, or lightly sautéed in oil. They are also added to stews and curries. The Japanese enjoy turnips carved in the shape of chrysanthemums and pickled and used as a garnish, boiled with a miso sauce; they use it in many recipes as a substitute for daikon.

'Tokyo Cross' turnips

55

WATER CHESTNUTS
(CHINESE WATER CHESTNUT)

Eleocharis dulcis

Mandarin: *ma tai;* **Japanese:** *kuwai*

FRESH WATER CHESTNUTS ARE crisper, nuttier, and sweeter than canned ones. They are the corms of attractive grassy, rushlike plants that grow to 3 feet tall in bogs or water gardens.

How to grow: Water chestnuts are easy to grow, especially if you have a water garden. They are not hardy but, if given winter protection, they can be grown in most areas. Plant water chestnut corms in large plastic containers filled with ordinary topsoil; submerge in a shallow pool. Make sure the water level in the tub remains at least 1 inch above soil level. Use a type of fertilizer recommended for water plants. Water chestnuts have few pests and diseases and mature in 6 months.

To harvest, lift the containers out of water when foliage dies. Remove whole plants from the container. Wash the mud off and harvest the chestnuts, putting some of them aside for next year's crop. Replant the corms with fresh soil. Keep moist throughout the winter in a dark, cool place. In areas where corms will not freeze, return them to the garden immediately.

To preserve harvested water chestnuts, store them in damp sand for a few months or peel and freeze them.

Varieties

Water chestnuts are usually available in Chinese grocery stores, but sometimes they won't sprout. The surest way to get viable corms is to order them in the spring from Van Ness Water Garden.

How to prepare: Peel the corms and use whole or sliced in any recipe calling for canned water chestnuts. Simply peel them and blanch for 10 minutes in boiling water before adding them to stir-fries, salads, and soups. Water chestnuts retain their crunch when cooked. In Thailand, they are a common ingredient in desserts, usually dressed with a sweet coconut milk sauce.

Plant water chestnuts in rich organic soil in a plastic container *(above)*. Place the tubers just barely under the soil. Gently water the tubers so as to not disturb the soil. Then lower the container into a shallow pond positioned so the chestnuts are a few inches below the water level *(below)*.

Water chestnuts

WINTER MELON
(WAX GOURD)

Benincasa hispida
Cantonese: *tung kwa;* **Mandarin:** *dong gwa;* **Japanese:** *tougan*

WINTER SQUASH
(JAPANESE PUMPKIN)

Cantonese: *nam kwa;* **Japanese:** *kabocha*

WINTER MELONS WEIGH IN at 25 pounds and, at maturity, develop a waxy outer layer. Their close relative, fuzzy melon, is a light green, medium sized squashlike vegetable covered with fuzz. Fuzzy melon is grown in the same manner as winter melon, except it is harvested when immature.

Winter squash is similar to Western winter squash; in fact, many popular varieties of the latter are bred in Japan.

How to grow: Winter melons and winter squash are grown in a similar manner and under the same conditions as cucumbers (see above). Hot-weather annuals, they mature in about 150 days. Both are large plants that usually ramble over the ground and are planted about 8 feet apart. They are heavy feeders and prone to a number of the same pests as cucumbers.

Winter melons may be harvested at any stage—from very immature to mature. Mature winter melons can be stored in a cool area for 3 months. Fuzzy melon is primarily eaten in its immature stage, at about 6 inches long. Winter squash must be allowed to fully

ripen to develop its rich flavor and color. Wait until the vines die down before harvesting.

Varieties

Winter melon is carried by Stokes, Nichols, Kitazawa, and Evergreen, and Johnny's carries a large selection of Japanese winter squash.

Winter Squash

The following were all bred in Japan and have dense, sweet flesh.

'Red Kuri' (Orange Hokkaido, Baby Red Hubbard): 92 days; orange, teardrop-shaped squash

'Sweet Mama': 85 days; green; squat shape; 2 to 3 pounds; dense; one of the best

'Sweet Dumpling': 100 days; green and white stripes; squat shape; small (4 inches)

How to prepare: In China, the white-fleshed winter melon is usually served as a soup. It can be cut up, but for festive occasions, it is usually

Asian squash and winter melon *(in back);* 'Sweet Mama' *(left);* 'Red Kuri' and two squash from the Asian market.

steamed whole. The top is cut off, seeds are removed, and stock is poured into the cavity. The melon is set in a pan and steamed for hours. Cooks then add mushrooms, vegetables, and seasonings to the soup. To serve, you reach into the melon and carve off a bit of the side with each serving.

The flavor of fuzzy melon is similar to that of a mild zucchini and it's mostly used in soups and pork and chicken stir-fries. Before using, peel off the fuzz.

Winter squash, a native of North America, is gaining in popularity in Asia—especially in Japan, where it is most commonly braised in a dashi stock (see recipe, page 73) or added to soups. In China, it is stir-fried with pork and mushrooms or made into a savory soup with pork or fish. In Thailand, cooks braise winter squash in coconut milk with lots of seasonings.

cooking from the
asian
garden

anging side by side in my pantry are a cast-iron frying pan and a wok—both utensils blackened with use. When I set up housekeeping in the early 1960s, I had never seen a wok, but once I became familiar with it, I made it one of my best-used tools. Other Asian influences gradually found their way into my kitchen as well. Stir-frying ranks with soup at the top of my list of ways to prepare garden vegetables. Japanese noodles fried with cabbage, and carrots and chicken soup with chive dumplings and pac choi, are family favorites. In recent years, my constant exposure to Asian vegetables has led me to consider pac choi, bunching onions, fresh ginger, pea pods, and fresh coriander as reliable staples.

In introducing Asian cooking, it is important to point out that its day-to-day style differs quite sharply from what Americans generally think of as Asian fare. Consider that Asians rarely know how Americans really eat at home—they think we live on hamburgers and French fries and remain unaware of the corn on the cob and zucchini bread that enrich our lives—and you start to sense how bound we are to stereotypes. I myself, who was raised on chop suey and bottled curry

powder, for instance, was surprised to learn that these "Asian foods" were mere anglicized creations. Further, I discovered that even the Asian food we eat in restaurants distorts our view, as these dishes are first, tailored to American tastes, and second, represent Asian restaurant rather than home-style cooking.

The fact is, well-meaning Chinese chefs, wanting to please their guests, often use more meat and oil in the United States than they would in China. And because Asian vegetables often are either unavailable or unfamiliar to Americans, many Chinese chefs limit their use to just a few dishes, incorporating only some of their cabbage-family greens and none of the fresh ginger shoots or Chinese chives enjoyed in China. Japanese chefs here, who are usually unable to obtain a full array of Japanese herbs and, again, are catering to American tastes, tend to avoid using seaweed and daikon. Even

Tempura vegetables and a lovely Thai squid salad, filled with fresh herbs, are two great Asian dishes.

recipes in most Asian cookbooks aimed at American cooks reflect this bias not only by including few vegetable dishes but by routinely substituting American vegetables for Asian ones in recipes.

Significantly, gardeners can view the food of Asia differently. We need not be limited by the supermarket or by the restaurateur's hopes of pleasing a timid, habit-bound clientele. Rather, we have the luxury of exploring Asian cuisines by growing the vegetables and herbs native to them. Of course, a thorough summary of Asian vegetable cookery in the few pages available here is impossible. The subject is enormous, not only because of the many nationalities involved but also owing to the vastly different climates, from the tropics to the mountains, encompassed by the continent. Here, I focus on Chinese and Southeast Asian cooking. You will find some information on Japan, Korea, and India and summaries of their cooking styles, but Chinese, Thai, and Vietnamese food dominate because, of all Asian food cultures, they incorporate the greatest array of vegetables and herbs gardeners can grow and enjoy.

Though Asia has long supported vast populations, only a small part of the land supports agriculture. Out of necessity, then, Asian cooks have had to maximize the use of their food, energy, and water, and this need has led to many similarities among cuisines. For instance, oven cooking, which is fuel-intensive, is found in none of these countries. Grazing land is limited, so the flesh of large grazing animals is rarely used. Food itself is dear, so,

when possible, all edible parts of both plants and animals are used. Until recently, the lack of refrigeration, too, forced a reliance on pickled and dried foods. Foods are pickled either by salt curing or in vinegar. At first taste, these vegetables can be too strong for Western palates, but within the context of Chinese cooking in general and, in particular, along with the often neutral components of a Japanese meal, they can provide an enjoyable tang.

Also common in much of Asia but foreign to most Westerners are dried foods such as shrimp and pac choi. These flavors might be compared to that of raisins in contrast to the flavor of fresh grapes; the original taste is intensified and altered in subtle ways. When you open a package of dried shrimp, the strong smell could discourage you but, once cooked and combined with other ingredients, the shrimp has quite a subtle taste. (For comparison's sake, think of the strong flavor of dried Parmesan cheese when tasted alone.)

A discussion of Asian foods would be incomplete without coverage of their healthfulness. You are surely aware by now of the campaign against saturated fat and for fiber in the diet. In this regard, Asian cooking ranks high among cooking styles. The cooking oils are predominantly vegetable based, myriad vegetables make up a large part of most meals, and protein sources are lean, as in the case of tofu. So, unlike far too many of life's pleasures, authentic Asian food is good for you.

Asian Cuisines

As Asia is so large and the cultures so varied, it helps to concentrate on a few of the cuisines in detail.

Chinese Cooking

Chinese cooking is a rich cuisine for the gardener-cook because many of the Chinese cooking techniques treat vegetables beautifully. Be warned, however: the range of ingredients and style in Chinese cooking is enormous. Cooks in northern China make dishes and use vegetables that their neighbors to the south have never heard of, and the opposite is true as well.

In China, food is one of the major components of the culture. In fact, discussing China's cooking without considering the philosophical and medicinal aspects of the food is something like taking a diamond out of its setting: the stone is wonderful to look at, but its true potential is hard to experience. For thousands of years, Chinese poets and philosophers have expounded on foods and food preparation. Each holiday, each event in a person's life, is associated with specific foods. But the cultural significance of food in China has long been matched by the minute attention paid to its nutritional properties. Food itself has always been treated as an integral part of personal health care. In fact, during some of the ancient dynasties, physicians who specialized in nutrition were among the highest-ranking doctors, and foods we now describe as high in vitamins and minerals were often prescribed for specific conditions—iron-rich foods following childbirth, for example.

Daily fare in China consists of rice served with vegetable-based dishes in which meat or seafood is used primarily as a seasoning. Thus, stir-fries of greens or beans might contain pork, chicken, or shrimp, but only in small amounts. There might be meat in the stock base of a braised vegetable dish or in a stew with vegetables.

Throughout most of China, the myriad members of the cabbage family are the primary vegetables. Also common is a wide variety of squash and beans. Ginger, garlic, and onions are the basic seasonings. The use of herbs is unusual, as these are considered medicinal, not culinary. But Chinese food draws intense flavors from dried mushrooms, seafood, and fruits; sauces made from seafood, beans, and fruits; pickled vegetables, and soy sauce. Many wheat breads and noodles are consumed in China, especially in northern areas, but rice is the predominant grain, and in much of China it is served at least once, in some form, every day.

Japanese Cooking

Limited agricultural soil and proximity to the ocean have greatly influenced the tastes of Japan. Japanese cuisine, elegant and highly stylized, is characterized by the use of dashi (a light bonita stock), a variety of braised and one-pot dishes, sea vegetables, a distinct scarcity of fats, and elegant presentation. While the Japanese enjoy many meat dishes, the primary pro-

teins are some form of soybean and seafood. As to vegetables, a somewhat limited range is widely used in numerous variations. Most often, vegetables appear in braised dishes, served cold with a dressing of some sort, or as pickles, which in some of their many forms are served with practically every meal. Rice and noodles are the primary starches; seasonings include ginger and onion plus numerous herbs, some of which are native to Japan.

In Japan, as perhaps no other country, the visual presentation of the meal has the aesthetic value of high art. A simple, clear soup might be garnished with chrysanthemum petals or a perfect leaf of mitsuba. The love of nature is often expressed in this medium—with daikon carved in the shape of a crane, for example, or layers of onion shaped into a calla lily. Table settings, too, are carefully thought out. For instance, a simple plate might contain nothing but a few slices of crab-stuffed cucumber and a sprig of red perilla. Appreciating the appearance of the food is an integral part of enjoying a meal in Japan.

In the garden, American gardener-cooks can give themselves access to Japanese herbs, the versatile daikon, and Japanese-bred cucumbers and squash. And by viewing the garden through Japanese eyes, Americans can renew their appreciation for the seasonal nature of gardening.

Indian Cooking

Indian cooks are the world's "flavorists." Instead of boiled potatoes with

butter, consider potatoes cooked with mustard seeds, ground cumin seeds, coriander, freshly grated ginger, red chilies, peanuts, and lemon juice—wonderful! Served with chapatis, an unleavened whole-wheat bread, and raita, a yogurt dish made with shredded cucumbers, this dish is close to heaven.

In many parts of India, the people are vegetarian; in others, they eat some meats and seafoods. Dahl—a loose term covering various legumes such as dried split peas and lentils—and milk products, including yogurt, are primary protein sources, particularly for the vegetarian segment of the population. Vegetables common in India include eggplants, potatoes, beans, carrots, cauliflower, okra, peas, and many kinds of dried legumes. The pancake-like chapati is served with most stewed dishes and soups. Rice, often mixed with spices and vegetables, is common throughout most of the country.

Southeast Asian Cooking

The foods of Southeast Asia are heavily influenced by their proximity to China and India, which means most meals include rice; stir-fries and flavorful curries are common, and recipes are commonly seasoned with coriander, ginger, shallots, and garlic. The primary protein sources are seafood and, in some countries, pork. In contrast to practice in China and India, most cultures use coconut milk in sauces, curries, and/or desserts, peanuts are often part of a flavoring paste, and fish sauces are a common

Ingredients

Purchase most of your ingredients in an Asian grocery store, in a natural-food store, or obtain them from mail-order sources. See the Resources section for more information.

Cooking Oils

Peanut oil and salad oils are used for frying. Sesame oil, with its strong characteristic flavor, is used in China and Japan as a seasoning rather than a cooking oil and is usually added to the dish at the last moment. In India, vegetable oils and, occasionally, ghee (clarified butter) are used in many curries and vegetable dishes.

Dried Ingredients

Mushrooms are one of the most important dried ingredients in both Chinese and Japanese cooking; they impart their rich, musky flavor to many dishes. Dried shrimp, fish, seaweed, and pork flavor soups and stir-fries. Most dried ingredients need to be reconstituted in water for a half hour before use. Use the liquid in a cooked dish.

Pickled Foods

Pickled foods are highly appreciated in all of Asia. In Japan, in particular, some meals are simply not complete without the accompaniment of a specific kind of pickle. You can make many of these traditional pickles from your garden produce; see the recipes on pages 63–65.

seasoning. People in this part of the world, unlike in China, use numerous fragrant fresh herbs for seasoning, including lemon grass, lime leaf, basils, and mints. Spicy dishes filled with chilies are not unusual.

Of course, there are differences among the cuisines. For example, in Vietnam, once a French colony, baguettes are common and often filled with sliced meats, vegetables, and herbs. Thai cooks are famous for their intricately carved vegetables and complex curries, and Indonesians enjoy many sambals (fiery pastes and condiments with seasonings unique to some areas).

Sauces and Condiments

For many Asian dishes, characteristic flavor lies in certain sauces. Key ingredients are oyster and hoisin sauces for Chinese food; Thai and Vietnamese fish sauces; and rice vinegar, sake, miso, and dashi for Japanese cooking. In *The Modern Art of Chinese Cooking,* Barbara Tropp gives detailed information on how to select and use the best of many kinds of Asian seasonings. She recommends both specific brands of these products and local sources all over the country.

Soy Sauce

Soy sauce is a pungent, salty brown liquid made from fermented soybeans, wheat, yeast, and salt. As a rule, Chinese cooks use the dark types for color and the lighter ones for salting dishes. Japanese cooks—who will alternately refer to this sauce as *tamari* or *shoyu*—generally use light to medium strengths of soy sauce. A good brand, available in most areas of this country, is the familiar Kikkoman, a medium-strength soy sauce.

Tofu

Tofu, also called bean curd, is a neutral-tasting, custardlike substance made from the curds of soybean milk. The greatest virtues of tofu are its nutritional richness and its ability to absorb flavors. Tofu comes in a range of textures, from silken to extra-firm. Silken tofu is wonderful whipped into desserts such as puddings and pies. The medium firmness, or what I call

"regular" is available in most American grocery stores.

Regular tofu, which is ready to use as is or cooked, keeps for four to five days in the refrigerator if rinsed in fresh water daily. Some recipes call for frozen tofu—which is chewier and more porous than fresh—because it soaks up flavor and marinades and gives a meatier texture in the final dish. Standard procedure for fresh tofu is to drain it, sliced, in a colander or on paper towels for half an hour prior to cooking. Simply cut the drained tofu into bite-size pieces or strips and toss it into a soup, stir-fry, or egg dish.

Condiments

Pickled Daikon and Carrots

Both Helen Chang and Mai Truong have helped me make these pickles. Pickling daikon in this manner is traditional in many parts of Asia. In China, these pickles might be part of a farmer's lunch, served with rice and a vegetable stir-fry. In Vietnam, showing the influence of the French, the slices might be used in a sandwich with liverwurst, head cheese, and herbs, or served with noodles and fragrant herbs. In Japan, they would be part of a selection of pickles offered as condiments at a meal.

If you prefer a crisp pickle, parboil the daikon and carrots in a quart of boiling water into which 1/2 teaspoon of alum has been added. See the recipe for pickled mustard on page 65 for more information on alum.

1 pound white daikon radish, (12 to
16 inches long, 2 inches in
diameter)

1 medium carrot

2 teaspoons salt

1/2-inch slice fresh ginger root

1/2 cup rice wine vinegar

1/2 cup sugar

Peel the daikon and carrots and cut them into 1/4" x 3" julienne strips. Put the vegetables in a medium bowl and sprinkle the salt over them. Crush the ginger slice with the back of a cleaver and add it to the vegetables. Stir the daikon and carrots with your hands to disperse the salt evenly. Set the bowl aside and let it sit at room temperature for one hour.

Drain the vegetables and then, using your hands, gently squeeze them to remove more of the liquid. Add the vinegar and sugar to the vegetables and stir until thoroughly mixed. Set aside to marinate at room temperature for 2 hours. Drain the mixture and remove the ginger and discard it. Put the pickled vegetables in a tight-sealing container and refrigerate until use. These pickles keep refrigerated for up to 2 weeks.

Makes about 2 cups.

Daikon Spicy Relish

This Japanese relish is a great accompaniment to grilled fish or marinated firm tofu. A little goes a long way, as it is spicy. Because you'll be stuffing the daikon, straight (rather than curved) chile peppers are easiest to use.

5 thin, dried red chile peppers

1 piece white daikon radish, about
5 inches long

Clockwise from top left: pickled daikon and carrots; daikon spicy relish; picked mustard, before and after; and slices of fresh Red Meat daikon with sugar.

Remove the stems and tops from the peppers. Remove the seeds by rolling each pepper between your fingers to loosen the seeds, then remove them. Peel the daikon and with a sharp chopstick or an ice pick puncture the sliced end of the daikon about 2 inches deep in 5 places. Force a pepper into each hole. (If the peppers are hard to get in, slice them in half and use the chop stick to work a half in each hole.)

Let the stuffed daikon rest for 5 minutes to soften the chiles. Grate 2 inches of the stuffed daikon over a bamboo rolling mat or cheesecloth. (You need the daikon to be at least 5 inches long to protect your knuckles from the grater.) The remaining 3

inches of daikon can be sliced and added to a soup. Get rid of some of the moisture in the grated daikon by rolling the bamboo mat over and squeezing or by wringing the cheesecloth. Serve the relish at once in an individual serving dish so each diner can season his or her own meal.

Makes $^1/_2$ cup, serves 4 to 6.

Pickled Ginger (Gari)

Pickled ginger is most popular in Japan invariably accompanying sushi and sashimi. The commercially prepared pickles often have added red food coloring but traditionally it is colored with red shiso leaves (perilla) as it is here.

$^1/_4$ pound young ginger root

$^1/_4$ cup rice vinegar

2 tablespoons mirin

2 tablespoons sake

2 tablespoons sugar

6 red shiso leaves

In a small saucepan, bring the rice vinegar, mirin, sake, and sugar to a gentle boil. Stir until the sugar dissolves. Cool the liquid.

Bring a small pot of water to a boil. Brush the ginger under running water, slice thinly, and then blanch slices for one minute. Drain the ginger and then transfer it into a sterilized half-pint canning jar, layering it evenly with the whole shiso leaves. Pour the cooled liquid over the ginger. Cover and let marry for 3 days in the refrigerator before serving. The ginger will keep in the refrigerator for up to 1 month.

Makes $1/2$ pint.

Pickled Mustard

Pickled mustard is a staple in much of Asia. Mai Truong helped me make it the way her Vietnamese mother taught her. Small amounts of the mustard are used to add flavor to stir-fries. It can be eaten over rice for a simple meal, or enjoyed as a condiment. Alum is used to make the pickle crunchier and to retain some of the green color but it is not a critical ingredient. You can get alum at pharmacies and Asian grocery stores. If you can't make your own, you can buy pickled mustard in the refrigerated section of most Asian markets.

    3 quarts water
    1/2 cup kosher salt
    4 cups sugar
    2 large Chinese mustards (look for
        solid-hearted varieties such as
        Amsoi)
    1 teaspoon solid alum (or 1/2 tea-
        spoon powdered alum)

Bring the water to a boil; add the salt and sugar. Stir until the salt and sugar have dissolved. Cool the liquid to room temperature.

Wash the mustard and cut a slit a few inches deep in the large base so the pickling liquid can penetrate the flesh. In a large pot, bring about 4 quarts of water to a rolling boil. Add the alum. Blanch the mustard for about 30 seconds. Drain and cool the mustard to room temperature.

Put the mustard into a large plastic container that can be sealed. Pour the pickling liquid over the mustard; make sure the entire surface is submerged. (If you don't have enough, make up more pickling liquid and add it.) Put the mustard in a cool, dark place to pickle for a week. The pickled mustard keeps in the refrigerator for a few weeks.

Makes 6 cups or about 1 $1/2$ pounds.

Tea

Lemon Grass Tea

Lemon grass makes a sprightly herb tea. Here, it is made with palm sugar (available from Asian grocery stores), but it is also pleasant with standard white sugar. For a variation try adding a little chopped ginger root.

    1/2 cup thinly sliced fresh lemon
        grass
    2 to 3 tablespoons palm sugar (or
        white sugar)
    1 quart cold water

Place the lemon grass and the palm sugar in the bottom of a teapot. Bring the water to a boil and pour it into the teapot over the lemon grass. Let the tea steep for at least 10 minutes. Pour the tea through a strainer and into teacups.

Serves 4.

Chrysanthemum Tea

This tea is famous in China and often served with dim sum.

    4 tablespoon dried chrysanthemum
        flowers
    1 quart cold water

Place the dried chrysanthemum flowers (shungiku) in the bottom of a teapot. Bring the water to a boil and pour it over the chrysanthemum flowers. Let the tea steep for at least 10 minutes. Pour the tea through a strainer and into tea cups.

Serves 4.

Steamed Rice

Steamed white rice is basic to all of Asia. In China and Japan they use short-grain rice. In India, however, they commonly use a long-grain, or fragrant basmati rice. The following recipe is the most basic and applicable to most white rice varieties. If you use a rice cooker, follow the proportions and directions that come with it. An interesting variation, and one packed with nutrition, is to make the rice with fresh green soybeans. The beans will cook in the same amount of time as the rice.

> 1 1/2 cups white rice
>
> 2 cups water
>
> Optional: 1 cup shelled green soy-
> beans

Rinse the rice under running water, then drain and place in a pot with a tight-fitting lid. (If using, add the optional green soybeans to the rice at this point.) Cover and bring to a boil. Reduce the heat to low and simmer for 15 minutes. Turn off the heat (don't lift the lid!) and let it sit covered for another 15 minutes. Fluff lightly and then serve.

Serves 4.

Shanghai Pac Choi Stir-fry

This recipe is a variation on one given to me by my wonderful neighbor, Helen Chang. Tatsoi, or the large types of pac choi, can be substituted for the Shanghai variety.

> 1 1/2 tablespoons vegetable oil
>
> 3 slices of fresh ginger root (1/8-
> inch thick), peeled and finely
> diced
>
> 1 pound Shanghai pac choi, cut
> diagonally into 1-inch pieces,
> white stems separated from the
> greens
>
> 1 1/2 to 2 tablespoons oyster sauce

Pour the oil into a wok. Heat over high heat until very hot. Add the ginger and stir-fry quickly until lightly brown. Add the white stems from the pac choi and stir-fry for 2 minutes. Add the greens and continue to stir-fry for 2 or 3 minutes more until the pac choi is tender but still slightly crunchy. Add the oyster sauce and stir to combine and bring the mixture to serving temperature.

Serves 3 to 4 as a side dish.

Carrot and Garlic Stir-fry

This popular vegetable stir-fry contrasts sweet and hot. Its richness combines well with other dishes containing the cool flavors of pac choi, cabbage, or spinach.

1 ½ tablespoons vegetable oil
1 pound carrots, peeled and cut
    into coins (about 3 cups)

2 large garlic cloves, peeled and
    minced
2 green onions, sliced thinly
¼ teaspoon hot red pepper flakes
¼ teaspoon salt
1 to 2 tablespoons chopped fresh
    coriander leaves
Garnish: coriander leaves

Pour the oil into a wok. Heat over high heat until very hot. Add the carrots and stir-fry for 3 or 4 minutes, add the garlic and green onions and stir to mix. Continue to stir-fry until the carrots are tender but still slightly crunchy. Add the red pepper, salt, coriander and mix. Taste and adjust the seasonings if necessary. To serve, pour contents of wok onto a small platter and garnish with cilantro leaves. Serve at once.

Serves 3 to 4 as a side dish.

Shishito Pepper and Eggplant Stir-fry with Beef

I learned about cooking baby Japanese eggplants and using mioga ginger blossoms from a woman selling both at the local farmer's market. Serve this dish with a vegetable stir-fry and rice cooked with soybeans (see the recipe on page 66) for a complete meal.

For the marinade:

1 tablespoon dry sherry
2 tablespoons soy sauce
1 tablespoon cornstarch
1/2 teaspoon sugar
1/2 pound beef filet strips

For the stir-fry:

2 tablespoons peanut oil
8 to 10 ounces Japanese baby eggplants, or larger eggplants cut into small strips
1 medium onion, chopped
16 green Shishito peppers or 1 sweet green Italian frying pepper cut into small strips
16 red Shishito peppers or 1 sweet red Italian frying pepper cut into small strips
6 mioga ginger blossoms, quartered (optional)
2 garlic cloves, minced
2 tablespoons fresh coriander leaves, chopped
2 teaspoons grated fresh ginger root
2 tablespoons oyster sauce
1/2 to 3/4 cups chicken broth
1/2 teaspoon hot red pepper flakes

To make the marinade:

In a small bowl, combine the sherry, soy sauce, cornstarch, and the sugar. Stir until the cornstarch is completely dissolved. Add the beef strips, toss, and set aside.

To make the stir-fry:

Over high heat in a nonstick wok, heat the peanut oil until it is very hot. Add the eggplants and stir-fry over high heat for 3 minutes. Add the onion, green and red peppers, and ginger blossoms; stir-fry 2 more minutes. Toss in the minced garlic, coriander, and grated ginger; cook for a couple of seconds. Put on a plate and set aside.

Heat the wok again, adding a little more peanut oil if necessary, and stir-fry the marinated beef for 1 minute or until medium rare. Return the vegetables to the wok, and then stir in the oyster sauce, the chicken broth, and the red pepper flakes. Heat together for another minute, and then serve the stir-fry at once over rice.

Serves 4.

Pickled Mustard Stir-fry with Pork

Mai Truong, who grew up in Vietnam, shared with me her favorite dish using pickled mustard—in this case with pork. I've also enjoyed adding shredded bamboo shoots, pea pods, and carrots to this recipe. Serve this dish with rice and soy sauce. For a complete meal accompany it with another stir-fry and a light soup. If you can't make your own, pickled mustard is available in the refrigerated section of most Asian markets.

1/2 pound lean pork, cut in thin strips across the grain

1/8 teaspoon salt

6 garlic cloves, minced, divided

1 pound pickled mustard (see recipe on page 65)

2 tablespoons vegetable oil

Fresh coriander leaves, chopped

Fresh green onions, chopped

Sprinkle the pork strips with the salt and half the minced garlic. Marinate the mixture for about 1 hour. Drain the pickled mustard and chop it into 1-inch pieces. In a hot wok heat the oil.

Sauté the remaining garlic until it is starting to turn golden. Add the pork strips and stir-fry until the meat turns gray. Add the pickled mustard and 1/2 cup of water. Cook for 3 more minutes, transfer to a warm platter and garnish the dish with coriander and green onions.

Serves 4.

Bitter Melon with Beef Stir-fry

Bitter flavors are an acquired taste, but if you enjoy bitter beer and radicchio you'll probably delight in this rich and complex dish. Serve it with steamed rice.

1 tablespoon dry sherry

1 tablespoon soy sauce

1 tablespoon cornstarch

1/2 pound beef tenderloin, cut in thin strips across the grain

1 pound bitter melon

1/2 teaspoon salt

1 red bell pepper

2 tablespoons peanut oil, divided

2 garlic cloves, minced

1 tablespoon grated fresh ginger root

2 tablespoons black bean sauce

2 teaspoons sugar

Garnish: 2 tablespoons of chopped fresh coriander leaves

Combine sherry, soy sauce, and cornstarch in a small bowl. Add the beef strips, coat thoroughly and set aside. Cut the bitter melon lengthwise; remove inside pulp and seeds. Slice thinly. Put into a bowl and sprinkle with salt. Let the melon sit for 20 minutes to remove some of the bitterness. After 20 minutes, squeeze out the water. Cut the red pepper in thin slices.

In a hot wok, heat one tablespoon of the oil. Add the bitter melon, garlic, and ginger and stir-fry for about 3 minutes. Remove the vegetables and put them on a warm serving plate. Add the remaining tablespoon of oil to the wok, heat and then add the beef strips. Stir over high heat until meat starts to brown but is still pink inside. Add the marinating juices, bean sauce, 1 cup water, and the sugar. Cook for one more minute, but do not overcook. Arrange the beef strips over the vegetables on the platter. Garnish with chopped coriander.

Serves 4.

Pea Shoots with Crab Sauce

Pea shoots are a special vegetable and greatly enjoyed in China. Here is an elegant pairing with crab.

For the sauce:

2 garlic cloves, minced

1 tablespoon vegetable oil

1 tablespoon cornstarch

1 cup chicken stock

2 tablespoons sherry

$^1/_2$ pound cooked crabmeat (about 1 cup)

$^1/_4$ cup chopped, blanched Chinese leek leaves or 1 tablespoon chopped fresh Oriental chive leaves

Salt

For the pea shoots:

1 tablespoon sesame oil

1 quart coarsely chopped fresh pea shoots

To make the sauce: In a saucepan over low heat, sauté the garlic in the vegetable oil until tender, about 1 minute. In a small bowl, blend the cornstarch with the chicken stock and sherry. Add the mixture to the pan and heat, stirring constantly until the sauce is thickened. Add the crabmeat and the Chinese leeks and simmer for another minute. Remove from the heat, and add salt to taste.

To make the pea shoots: In a wok or large pan, heat the sesame oil and stir-fry the pea shoots for about 3 minutes or until just tender. Lightly toss them with the sauce and serve them over steamed rice.

Serves 4.

Stir-fried Shrimp and Greens

David Cunningham, one time staff horticulturist at the Vermont Bean Seed Company, created this recipe to take advantage of his many Asian greens. Serve this stir-fry with steamed rice.

For the shrimp marinade:

1 tablespoon tomato paste

1 tablespoon cornstarch

1 tablespoon soy sauce

2 tablespoons vinegar

2 tablespoons water

1/2 teaspoon Chinese mustard

1 1/2 pounds raw shrimp, shelled, cleaned, and deveined

For the sauce:

1/2 cup chicken stock

1 tablespoon cornstarch

1 tablespoon soy sauce

2 teaspoons honey

4 large garlic cloves, minced

For the stir-fry

1/4 cup peanut oil, divided

2 large heads pac choi, stems sliced diagonally in 2-inch pieces

4 green onions, sliced diagonally

1 quart tatsoi leaves

To make the marinade: Mix the marinade ingredients together, add the shrimp, and refrigerate for 3 hours. Drain and reserve both the liquid and the shrimp.

To make the sauce: Mix the sauce ingredients together, add the drained marinade liquid and set aside.

To make the stir-fry: Heat the wok over high heat and add about half the oil. Stir-fry the shrimp quickly in small batches. As they are cooked, put the shrimp and any juices into a bowl and reserve.

Add the remaining oil and stir-fry the pac choi stems and green onions for about one minute. Add the tat soi leaves and stir until they are wilted. Add the sauce, lower the heat, and stir until thickened. Add the cooked shrimp together with their liquid. Heat all together while stirring, for another minute.

Serves 6 to 8.

Gai Lon with Bamboo Shoots and Barbecued Pork

Helen Chang helped me develop this recipe. She showed me how to prepare the gai lon by leaving only the rich tasting stalks and young buds. Purchase barbecued pork at gourmet and Asian markets. Accompany the stir-fry with rice, a light soup such as chive dumpling soup (see recipe on page 76), or other stir-fried dishes.

1 pound of gai lon (about 5 cups trimmed)

1/2 teaspoon salt

2 1/2 tablespoons peanut oil, divided

1/4 pound Chinese barbecued pork at room temperature, sliced thinly

3 slices fresh young ginger, or

2 slices mature ginger, 2 inches long, crushed slightly

2 green onions, white part only, chopped finely

1/2 cup fresh or frozen bamboo shoots, sliced thinly

2 tablespoons oyster sauce

Wash the gai lon well to remove any grit. Peel the skin of the largest stems and remove any large tough leaves. Cut the stalks into 3- or 4-inch lengths. Cut the widest stems lengthwise, so they cook in the same amount of time as the smaller pieces.

Bring a large pot of water to a boil; add 1/2 teaspoon of salt and then the gai lon and parboil for 1 1/2 minutes. Pour the gai lon into a colander and set aside to drain.

Heat the wok over high heat and when very hot add 1/2 tablespoon of oil and then add the pork and stir-fry for 30 seconds. Remove the pork to a plate. Add the remaining 2 tablespoons of oil, the ginger, and green onions and stir-fry for 30 seconds. Add the drained gai lon and the bamboo shoots and stir. Then, add the barbecued pork and the oyster sauce. Stir and cook until the gai lon is tender, about 2 more minutes. Transfer the mixture to a warm plate and serve with rice.

Serves 2 as a single entree with a soup. Serves 4 as part of a traditional Chinese meal combined with other stir-fry dishes.

Miso Soup

Miso soup is a traditional Japanese soup, eaten most often at breakfast. Miso paste is made from fermented soybeans and can be found in Asian and natural-food stores in plastic tubs. There are all different kinds of miso—ranging in color from blonde to rich reddish-brown—depending on the ingredients from which it is made, the length of the fermentation process, and season. Miso contains *acidophilus*—the "helpful" bacteria found in yogurt—which will perish if miso is boiled.

Some versions of this soup are made with *dashi* (bonito flake stock) and *kombu* (seaweed). The version that appears here is suited more to Western tastes and is a great way to get acquainted with this lovely soup. After you have made it a few times try adding some kombu and/or dashi to the simmering water—but be careful, as the flavor from these ingredients can overpower your soup. Put the dashi in cheesecloth and use it as a "teabag" to flavor your miso gently. Kombu contains agents that accelerate the softening of the soup's vegetables while they cook. If used, both the dashi and the kombu should be removed from the soup just before the water begins to boil.

1-inch piece of fresh ginger root, sliced
1 medium carrot, minced
4 ounces firm tofu, in 1/2-inch cubes
1/4 cup miso paste (more or less to taste)
2 scallions, minced

Bring one quart of water and the ginger slices to a boil. Simmer for 5 minutes, then remove the ginger. Add the minced carrot and tofu, and simmer for another 2 minutes. Take the soup off the stove and allow to cool for 1 to 2 minutes. Add the miso and stir gently until it dissolves. Scatter the minced scallion on top and serve immediately.

Serves 4.

Thai Chicken Soup with Pigeon Peas

This lovely light soup is a great beginning to a Thai meal or Chinese stir-fry. Some folks enjoy the fish sauce that gives an authentic Thai taste; others prefer to leave it out.

2 tablespoons vegetable oil

1 frying chicken (3 to 3 1/2 pounds), cut in 6 or 7 pieces

1 large onion, chopped

3 ribs celery, chopped

2 medium carrots, chopped

3 stalks lemon grass, chopped in 2-inch pieces and slightly crushed to release flavors

1 1/2 tablespoons grated fresh ginger root

4 garlic cloves, minced

4 leaves Kaffir lime leaf

3 whole dried chiles

1/2 teaspoon ground coriander seeds

Salt and freshly ground black pepper

2 cups shelled fresh pigeon peas or green peas (preferably fresh)

2 small green onions sliced thinly, including 1-inch of the greens

1/3 cup chopped fresh coriander leaves

1 tablespoon lime juice

Optional: 1 tablespoon Thai fish sauce

In a very large sauté pan, heat the oil on medium. Add a few chicken pieces and brown on all sides. Repeat the process with the remaining chicken. Transfer the browned chicken to a large soup pot. Pour off the excess fat from the pan and add the onions. Sauté until translucent, about 7 minutes. Add the onions to the chicken along with 2 quarts of water. Add the celery, carrots, lemon grass, ginger, garlic, lime leaf, chiles, and ground coriander and bring to the boil. Skim off and discard any foam, reduce the heat, then simmer for 45 minutes.

74

Pour the chicken and liquid through a colander. Pour the stock back into the soup pan and let the fat rise to the top. Skim off and discard most of the fat on the surface. Meanwhile, cool and separate the chicken meat from the bones and skin, and add the meat back to the stock. You should have about 3 cups of chicken meat.

Bring the soup back to a boil and add the pigeon peas and green onions and cook for about 5 minutes, just until the peas are tender. Add the coriander leaves, the lime juice, and the (optional) fish sauce to taste.

Daikon and Sparerib Soup

This recipe was given to me by Helen Chang. Growing up in Taiwan she remembers her mother making this soup often. Traditionally it is served along with the meal. When we first made it together I was surprised at how easy it was and how flavorful and mild the daikon became. When you buy the spareribs have the butcher cut them across the bones so they are in strips 1 1/2 inches wide.

3/4 pound pork spareribs, cut cross-
    wise
1 1/2-inch piece fresh ginger root,
    divided
3/4 teaspoon salt, divided
1 medium white daikon radish
    (about 16 inches long)
1 large carrot
1/8 cup dried scallops, in 1/2-inch
    cubes
1/4 cup Virginia ham, in 1/4-inch
    cubes
Pinch of white pepper

To prepare the pork, remove the membrane and extraneous fat from the back of the ribs. Cut the ribs apart between each rib to create pork rib sections about 1 1/2 inches in diameter.

Fill a medium saucepan with about 2 inches of water and bring it to a boil. Add a 1-inch piece of the ginger and 1/2 teaspoon of salt to the water and bring it back to the boil. Add the ribs and bring the water to boil once again. Simmer the ribs for three minutes and then drain and rinse in cold water to remove any scum. Discard the ginger and set the pork aside.

Bring 6 cups of water to a boil in the soup pot and add two 1/4-inch thick slices of ginger, the pork ribs, and the remaining 1/4 teaspoon of salt. Bring the mixture to a simmer and cook for 45 minutes.

In the meantime, prepare the vegetables. Peel the daikon and cut them into 1 1/2-inch oblique chunks. (You should have 2 1/2 to 2 3/4 cups of daikon.) Peel and cut the carrot into chunks. (You should have about 1 cup of cut carrot chunks.) Once the pork has simmered for 45 minutes add the daikon and carrots and simmer for 35 to 45 minutes longer, or until the carrots are tender and the daikon has turned translucent.

Once the vegetables are done, remove the pan from the heat and add the pepper and adjust the seasonings. Skim any excess fat from the surface and either serve immediately or refrigerate and reheat before serving.

Serves 4 to 6.

Dumpling Soup with Oriental Chives

This recipe was created by Helen Chang of Los Altos, California. A native of Taiwan, her version of this classic soup is light and savory and a marvelous way to use your harvest of Oriental chives. The dough for the dumplings can be purchased already prepared, in the produce or frozen food section of your supermarket, or in Asian markets. Sometimes they are called wonton skins, other times pasta wraps. You can easily substitute 1 large bunch of spinach for the pac choi greens.

For the dumplings:

- $1/3$ pound ground pork
- $3/4$ cup finely chopped green cabbage
- $1/3$ cup finely grated carrots
- $1/2$ cup finely chopped fresh Oriental chive leaves
- 4 tablespoons finely grated peeled fresh ginger root, divided
- 2 tablespoons chopped coriander leaves
- $1/2$ teaspoon freshly ground black pepper
- 1 teaspoon salt
- 1 teaspoon sugar
- 3 teaspoons cornstarch
- 1 egg, lightly beaten
- 1 (12-ounce) package of small square wonton skins, thawed if frozen

For the soup:

- 2 quarts chicken broth
- 10 to 12 mushrooms, thinly sliced
- 1 large head of pac choi, green leafy sections cut in narrow strips; large white stems reserved for another use
- Hot pepper sauce (optional)
- Garnish: 3 teaspoons chopped coriander leaves

To make the dumplings: In a medium bowl, place the pork, cabbage, carrots, chives, 2 tablespoons grated ginger, coriander leaves, pepper, salt, sugar, and cornstarch. Add the egg and stir to combine the ingredients.

Place the wonton skins, a few at a time, on a clean work surface. (Meanwhile, keep the rest of the wontons in the package, or place a slightly damp towel over them to prevent them from drying out.) Mound a teaspoon of filling in the middle of each wonton square and then fold to form a triangle or semicircle. Press the edges together to seal, then bend corners toward each other as you would for wontons. (Refer to the wonton package for folding directions.) Place the folded dumplings on a cookie sheet, leaving space between each one. Cover and refrigerate dumplings when filled, if not using immediately.

When ready to serve, bring a large pot of water to boil and add the dumplings and simmer for 5 to 6 minutes, or until they become translucent. Remove them from the water with a slotted spoon and divide them among 6 bowls.

To make the soup: In the meantime, pour the chicken broth into a large soup pot. Add the remaining 2 tablespoons of ginger. Bring to a simmer and add the mushrooms. Simmer over low to medium heat for one minute. Add the pac choi leaves and chives to the simmering broth. Add hot sauce to taste, if using.

To serve: Fill the bowls with broth and pac choi. Garnish each bowl of dumplings with chopped coriander.

Serves 6.

Henry's Salad with Vietnamese Coriander

Henry Tran is both a friend and landscaping contractor with whom I work. He has helped me identify a number of Vietnamese greens and herbs over the years and generously shared the traditional ways they are used in Vietnam. The following is one of his salad suggestions.

2 teaspoons sugar

1 small Vidalia, Maui, or other sweet white onion, sliced paper thin

2 tablespoons rice vinegar

2 teaspoons low-sodium soy sauce

1 teaspoon finely chopped fresh Vietnamese coriander

1/2 teaspoon finely chopped mint or spearmint

1/8 teaspoon hot red pepper flakes

Pinch of salt

1/8 teaspoon finely chopped fresh ginger root (optional)

6 cups butter lettuce, washed and dried

Garnish: 4 sprigs fresh Vietnamese coriander

Pour 1 1/2 cups of water into a medium bowl. Add the sugar and stir until it has dissolved. Separate the onions into rings and add them to the bowl. Allow the mixture to sit for 30 minutes.

In a small mixing bowl, combine the rice vinegar, soy sauce, Vietnamese coriander, mint, chile flakes, salt, and the ginger, if being used, to make the dressing.

In a large bowl, toss the lettuce with the dressing, coating the leaves well. Divide the lettuce among four plates. Drain the onions. Divide and place them atop each serving. Garnish each salad with a sprig of Vietnamese coriander.

Serves 4.

Vietnamese Salad Rolls (Goi Cuon)

This elegant recipe is a fabulous way to feature all your Southeast Asian herbs. It is a traditional dish and was given to me by Mai Truong, who grew up in Vietnam. It makes a great light first course or a special luncheon dish. Use leftover fish dipping sauce for a light salad dressing.

1 pound pork loin (or use leftover
    roasted or grilled pork loin)
16 to 20 medium raw shrimp
6 ounces fine rice vermicelli
1 large head leaf or butter lettuce
5 to 6 cups loosely packed fresh
    herb leaves including: mint, Thai
    basil, perilla leaves, rau ram,
    and cilantro
2 cups mung bean sprouts
1 12-ounce package of 11-inch egg
    roll wrappers (made with wheat
    flour, tapioca, and water)
1 large bunch garlic chive leaves
1 tablespoon hot chile paste

In a saucepan, bring a quart of water to a boil. Add the pork loin; cover and simmer on low heat for about 20 to 30 minutes or until tender. Drain and cool the pork. In another saucepan, bring 2 cups of water to a boil, add the shrimp and simmer on low for about 3 minutes. Drain and set them aside. In a third pot, bring a quart of water to a boil, add the vermicelli and cook for 3 minutes. Drain, rinse in cold water, and set aside.

Spicy Bean Sprouts

Many Asian cultures enjoy bean sprout salads. This is a spicy Korean version.

For the dressing:
1 tablespoon vegetable oil
2 teaspoons hot sesame oil
1 tablespoon toasted sesame
    seeds, ground
2 garlic cloves, minced
2 green onions, finely chopped
1/4 cup soy sauce
1 teaspoon sugar
1/2 teaspoon cayenne pepper
Garnish: 1 teaspoon whole toasted
    sesame seeds

For the salad:
1 pound fresh mung bean sprouts

To make the dressing: Combine all the ingredients in a small jar, cover and shake vigorously.

To make the salad: Carefully wash the bean sprouts. Bring 2 quarts of salted water to a rolling boil. Add the sprouts and cook them for 1 minute. Do not overcook, as the sprouts should remain crunchy. Drain and rinse with cold water. In a bowl, toss the sprouts with the dressing and chill for about 1 hour. Sprinkle with whole sesame seeds before serving.

Serves 4.

Before assembling the rolls, cut the pork into thin slices. Peel and devein the shrimp and slice each in half lengthwise. Wash and drain the lettuce and herbs. Place the pork, shrimp, vermicelli, lettuce leaves, herb leaves, and bean sprouts in bowls near a clean work surface.

Fill a large bowl with warm water and keep it at your work table. Dampen one egg roll wrapper at a time by dipping the edges into the warm water; place it on your work surface and dampen the middle by sprinkling it with water. Spread the moisture around with your fingers so the wrapper becomes evenly moist, but

not wet. Let the wrapper soften a few seconds. (The thickness of the salad rolls can vary—it depends on how much filling you put in. After you fill and roll a few you will determine the final size you prefer.)

To fill the first wrapper, spread several strands of noodles on it, 2 inches from the bottom. Cover with part of a lettuce leaf, a selection of 3 or 4 different herb leaves, a small amount of bean sprouts, and three slices of the pork on top of each other. Fold the bottom part of the wrapper over the ingredients and fold in both sides of the wrapper, as you would to make a burrito. Place 3 shrimp halves and 3 whole garlic

chive leaves on the top of the first roll of the wrapper, letting the chives stick out on one side. Finish rolling the wrapper up until it forms a cylinder. The shrimp will be visible from the outside through the wrapper. Repeat assembly for each roll.

Place the finished rolls on a serving platter and garnish, or make up individual plates of 2 or 3 rolls each. Accompany the rolls with a small bowl of hoisin dipping sauce, another small bowl of fish dipping sauce, and a bowl of the hot chile paste.

Makes 10 to 12 rolls, serves 4 to 6.

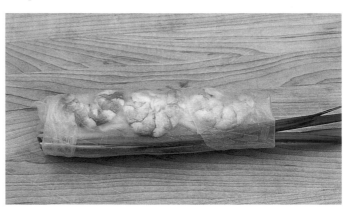

(Above, left) To roll the salad rolls, first place the ingredients on the damp wrapper a few inches from the bottom. *(Above, right)* Fold the bottom part of the wrapper over the ingredients, then bring over the sides. Place 3 shrimp in front of the rolled part and roll a half turn. *(Below, left)* Place a few chive leaves on the wrapper then roll another turn until the roll is finished *(below, right)*.

For the hoisin dipping sauce:

> 1/2 cup hoisin sauce
>
> 2 tablespoons water
>
> 1 tablespoon unsalted, dry-roasted
>   peanuts, finely chopped

Blend the hoisin sauce with the water. Put it in a small serving bowl and sprinkle with the chopped peanuts.

For the fish dipping sauce:

> 3 to 6 garlic cloves, minced
>
> 3 fresh serrano peppers, seeded
>   and minced
>
> 1/4 cup fresh lemon juice
>
> 1/3 cup Vietnamese fish sauce
>   (nuoc nam)
>
> 1/4 cup sugar

With a mortar and pestle, crush the garlic and peppers into a smooth paste. Put the lemon juice into a glass bowl,

add the garlic-pepper paste, fish sauce, sugar, and 3/4 cup warm water. Stir to combine. This dipping sauce can be kept in a jar in the refrigerator for several weeks.

Makes 1 1/2 cups.

Beef and Pork Japanese Vegetable Rolls

The Japanese have many elegant meat and vegetable combination appetizers and this is one.

For the sauce:

1/4 cup water

1 tablespoon sugar

1 tablespoon mirin

3 tablespoons soy sauce

For the rolls:

2 medium carrots (about 4 ounces)

1 burdock root (about 4 ounces)

1 tablespoon white vinegar

6 green onions

4 ounces yard-long beans

1 teaspoon soy sauce

10 ounces lean beef or pork, teriyaki style, and thinly sliced

2 tablespoons cornstarch

1 tablespoon vegetable oil

To make the sauce: Combine the water with the sugar, mirin, and soy sauce and set aside.

To make the rolls: Cut the carrots lengthwise into strips about 5 inches long and 1/4 inch square. Peel the skin off the burdock root and cut it into the same size strips as the carrots. To prevent discoloration, soak the burdock in water with the vinegar for 5 minutes. Cut the green onions and set them aside. Cut the yard-long beans into 5-inch lengths.

In a small saucepan, bring 1/4 cup water to a boil, add 1 teaspoon soy sauce, the carrots, and the burdock root. Simmer the vegetables for 5 minutes, drain them, and set aside. Parboil the beans in 2 cups of water for 3 minutes, cool them quickly under running cold water, drain them, and set them aside.

Spread the beef or pork slices on a cutting board and sprinkle them lightly with cornstarch.

To assemble: Put 2 pieces of each vegetable and green onions on a piece of meat and roll them up tightly. Secure the rolls with a wooden toothpick. When all the rolls are done, sprinkle them lightly with cornstarch.

To serve: In a nonstick frying pan, heat the vegetable oil and brown the rolls evenly on all sides. You may have to do this in 2 batches. Return all the rolls to the pan and pour the sauce over the rolls and simmer them for another 5 minutes, turning them in the sauce so they are evenly glazed. Serve on individual plates while still warm.

Serves 4.

Spinach Purée

This spinach recipe is typical of many recipes from India; it contains many complex flavors yet is surprisingly light.

> 3-inch piece fresh ginger root,
>   divided
> 3 green chiles, seeded and
>   membranes removed
> 1 pound fresh spinach, washed and
>   drained
> 3 tablespoons butter
> 1 small onion, minced
> 1/2 teaspoon salt
> Dash of freshly grated nutmeg
> Dash of cayenne pepper
> Garnish: shredded fresh ginger root

In a large pot, bring 1 cup of water to a boil. Slice off 2 inches of the ginger and add to the water. Shred the remaining ginger for the garnish. Chop the green chiles and add to the pot. Add the fresh spinach and cook for about 3 minutes. Drain the liquid and puree the mixture in a blender, and set aside.

In a pan, melt the butter and sauté the onion until it is soft. Add the puréed spinach to the onion and stir to combine. Season with salt, nutmeg, and cayenne pepper. Serve hot, garnished with shredded ginger.

Serves 4.

Edamame

This recipe was suggested to me by June Tachibana, who sells fresh soybeans at the Palo Alto farmer's market. She says this traditional Japanese snack is often enjoyed with beer. Salt helps keep the soybeans bright green.

> 2 tablespoons salt
> 1/2 pound fresh green soybeans,
>   pods on

Pour 2 quarts of water in a large saucepan and bring it to a boil. Add the salt and stir to dissolve. Add the soybeans and boil them for 4 to 6 minutes and until the beans are tender and still firm but not mushy. Drain the beans in a colander. Put the beans in a bowl and serve. Have snackers peel their own beans and provide them with an extra bowl for the empty pods.

Serves 2 as a snack.

Japanese Noodles

Noodles of many types are popular in Japan. I am most fond of the fresh noodles available in Asian grocery stores and usually keep some on hand. They are found in the refrigerator section and are sealed in plastic; they usually keep for a few months. Americans are most familiar with these ramen noodles in their dried form. The following is a much more satisfying dish than the dried commercial version and contains a lot more nutrition.

2 tablespoons corn oil

1 1/4 pounds fresh Japanese noodles

1/2 cup chopped pickled mustard (see the recipe on page 65, or buy it in an Asian market)

1 cup Chinese cabbage ribs, sliced

1 medium carrot, thinly sliced

1 large shallot or small onion, diced

4 cups Chinese cabbage leaves, chopped

1/2 cup chicken stock

1 tablespoon Worcestershire sauce

1/2 teaspoon chili powder

1/2 teaspoon sugar

1/2 teaspoon salt

Garnish: 1 sliced green onion

In a wok, heat the corn oil over high heat. Add the pickled mustard, ribs of Chinese cabbage, and sliced carrots. Stir-fry for 2 minutes. Add the shallot and the chopped leaves of the Chinese cabbage and stir-fry 1 minute more. Toss in the noodles and cook for 2 more minutes. Add the chicken stock, Worcestershire sauce, chili powder, sugar, and salt. Cook 1 minute more to combine the flavors. Serve in a bowl garnished with sliced green onion.

Serves 2.

Winter Squash, Japanese Style

Braising vegetables with dashi is a favorite Japanese way to cook many vegetables. If you are new to dashi and its taste of the sea, you might want to replace half the dashi with water. Dashi may be purchased in dried form in Asian markets. Note that the soy will darken the squash; if you wish to retain the color, add the soy sauce to the broth in the bottom of the serving bowl instead of during the cooking.

    1 pound winter squash, Japanese
        Kabocha or 'Red Kuri'
    3/4 cup reconstituted dashi
    2 1/2 tablespoons sugar
    1 tablespoon mirin
    1 tablespoon soy sauce

Wash the squash and cut it in half to remove the cubes. Cut it into 2-inch squares. Slice off the skin here and there to give the surface a mottled look and to enable the flavor of the broth to penetrate. Put the squash skin-side down in a saucepan, add the dashi, sugar and mirin. Cover and simmer for 7 to 8 minutes over medium heat. After 4 to 5 minutes turn the pieces over gently one by one. Add the soy sauce and continue to simmer 7 to 8 minutes more or until tender, turning the squash over once while simmering. Test for tenderness and remove the squash just as it softens. Serve hot or at room temperature.

Serves 4 as a side dish.

Green Beans with Sesame

This is a lovely side dish to accompany grilled tofu or fish and rice in a Japanese meal. The daikon pickles on page 63 would fill out the meal. Dashi can be purchased in dried form from Asian grocery stores. Nori is the flat, pressed seaweed sheets that are used to make sushi rolls. It can also be purchased at Asian grocery stores.

    Optional: 1 sheet of nori seaweed
    2 cups yard-long or standard green
        beans
    1/2 cup sesame paste
    1/2 cup basic dashi (made following
        the directions on the package)

3 teaspoons light soy sauce

4 teaspoons sugar

If using the nori, lightly toast the sheet in a dry frying pan. Take it out of the pan, cut it into narrow strips, and set it aside.

Boil the beans in slightly salted water until just tender. Drain and cool under cold running water. Cut the beans into 2-inch lengths. Mix the sesame paste, reconstituted dashi, soy sauce, and sugar to make a sesame dressing. Put the beans into 4 serving bowls, top each with a spoonful of the dressing and garnish with the shredded nori.

Serves 4 as a side dish.

Spicy Eggplant

This is a classic Indian treatment of eggplant filled with lots of fragrant spices. Serve with grilled meats, Indian flat bread or pita bread, and Raita.

For the Masala spice mixture:

1 1/2 teaspoons ground coriander

2 teaspoons ground cumin

1/2 teaspoon ground red pepper

1 bay leaf

1/8 teaspoon cinnamon

1/8 teaspoon freshly ground nutmeg

Dash of ground cloves

Dash of ground cardamom

For the eggplant:

1 pound eggplant (2 medium)

1 1/2 tablespoons vegetable oil

1 tablespoon butter

2 medium onions, finely chopped

Masala spice mixture

3 medium fresh tomatoes, peeled, seeded, and chopped

2 or 3 green chiles, seeded and chopped

Salt and freshly ground black pepper

1 tablespoon fresh chopped coriander

Combine the spices and set aside. Preheat a gas, electric, or charcoal grill. Cut the eggplants in half lengthwise and cut scores into the flesh, without cutting through the skin. Rub the eggplant halves with a little vegetable oil and grill until the skin blackens and the eggplants are soft. Cool, then peel, and chop the flesh coarsely.

In a medium pot, heat the remaining vegetable oil and the butter and sauté the onions until they are golden. Add the Masala spices and cook together for 1 minute. Add the tomatoes and green chiles and sauté for 3 more minutes. Remove and discard the bay leaf. Add the chopped eggplant and sauté until the mixture is dry and comes away from the sides of the pan. Add salt and freshly ground pepper to taste and garnish with the coriander leaves. Serve hot or at room temperature.

Serves 4.

Spicy and Sour Squid Salad

Chef Areeawn Fasudhani, of the Khan Toke Thai House in San Francisco, created this lovely dish. Note that *nam pla,* listed among the ingredients, is a salty fish sauce commonly used in Thai cooking. It is bottled like soy sauce and is available in Asian markets.

> 1/2 pound cleaned and sliced squid (about 1 cup)
>
> 1 tablespoon finely chopped lemon grass
>
> 2 tablespoons lime juice
>
> 1 1/2 tablespoons nam pla (Thai fish sauce)
>
> 1 tablespoon sliced shallots
>
> 1 teaspoon chili powder, or finely chopped hot peppers to taste
>
> 1 teaspoon finely chopped coriander root (if available)
>
> 1 teaspoon chopped green onions
>
> 1 teaspoon coriander leaves
>
> Lettuce or cabbage leaves
>
> 10 mint leaves
>
> Sprigs of fresh coriander

Dip the squid into boiling water for 30 seconds; drain, then put it in a bowl. Season with the lemon grass, lime juice, nam pla, shallots, chili powder, coriander root, green onions, and coriander leaves. Toss lightly. Place mixture on serving plate next to lettuce or cabbage; decorate with the mint and coriander leaves. Serve immediately. Eat by scooping up squid and juices together with the lettuce or cabbage leaves.

Serves 2 as salad or 4 as appetizer.

Shungiku Greens with Sesame Dressing

Cooked greens with a sesame dressing is a popular vegetable side dish in Japan. Serve the greens with grilled fish, rice, and one or two types of pickles for a typical Japanese meal.

For the dressing:

> 1 teaspoon toasted sesame seeds, ground
>
> 1 teaspoon sugar
>
> 2 tablespoons chicken stock
>
> 1/3 cup soy sauce

For the salad:

> 1 pound shungiku greens
>
> Garnish: 1 teaspoon toasted sesame seeds, whole

To make the dressing: Combine all the ingredients in a small jar, cover and shake vigorously.

To make the salad: Wash the shungiku greens and remove any thick stems. Bring 2 quarts of water to a rolling boil. Add the greens and cook for 1 minute. Drain and rinse with cold water. Press the water from the shungiku and put into a bowl. Dress the greens with the sesame dressing and sprinkle with whole, toasted sesame seeds.

Serves 4.

86

Gado-Gado

This is a classic Indonesian dish and has many variations. I like this one as it contains so many vegetables. It makes a wonderful vegetarian lunch.

For the sauce:

1 cup chunky peanut butter

3 garlic cloves, minced

3 to 5 chiles, minced

2-inch piece fresh ginger root, grated

1/3 cup soy sauce

1 teaspoon sugar

1 teaspoon salt

2 Kaffir lime leaves (fresh or dried)

1/4 cup fresh lime juice

For the vegetables:

3 cups yard-long beans, cut in 2-inch lengths

3 medium carrots, julienned

3 cups fresh spinach, loosely packed

3 cups chopped Chinese cabbage

2 cups fresh bean sprouts

3 tablespoons vegetable oil

5 ounces firm tofu

1/2 medium onion, thinly sliced

4 hard-boiled eggs

To make the sauce: In a pot, combine the peanut butter, garlic, chiles, ginger, soy sauce, sugar, salt, lime leaves, and 2 1/2 cups water. Bring the mixture to a boil and simmer, stirring often, for 30 minutes. Cool the sauce, stir in the fresh lime juice, and reserve.

To make the vegetables: In a large pot, bring 2 quarts of salted water to a rolling boil. Add the long beans and carrots and cook them for 2 minutes. Remove them from the cooking water with a slotted spoon, rinse with cold water, and set them aside. Bring the water to a boil again and blanch the spinach, Chinese cabbage, and bean sprouts for 30 seconds. Drain and set aside.

To serve: In a frying pan, heat the vegetable oil and fry the tofu on all sides until golden brown. Drain on a paper towel and set aside. Add the sliced onions to the same pan and fry over medium heat until golden. Drain them on a paper towel and reserve. Quarter the hard-boiled eggs. Slice the tofu 1/4 inch thick. In a serving bowl, toss the vegetables with the peanut sauce. Garnish with the sliced tofu, the quartered eggs and the fried onions.

Serves 4 to 6.

Thai Red Vegetable Curry

Red curry is one of the traditional dishes in Thailand. It is very spicy, and lush with coconut milk. Shrimp paste is available in Asian markets.

For the red curry paste:

    5 to 10 dried red chile peppers
    1 tablespoon cumin seeds
    1 teaspoon caraway seeds
    20 whole black peppercorns
    1 tablespoon whole coriander seeds
    4 Kaffir lime leaves (fresh or dried)
    3 shallots, minced
    6 garlic cloves, minced
    1 2 1/2-inch piece fresh ginger root,
        grated
    2 stalks lemon grass, finely minced
        (white part only)
    1/4 cup vegetable oil
    1 tablespoon fresh grated lime peel
    1 tablespoon shrimp paste

For the vegetable curry:

    3 carrots, peeled and thinly sliced
    2 cups snow peas, strings and
        stems removed
    1 cup peeled white daikon radish,
        cut into julienne strips
    6 baby turnips
    1 cup broccoli, in small florets
    2 cups chopped Chinese cabbage
    1 cup tatsoi leaves
    1 cup chopped pac choi
    1 cup chopped mustard greens
    1/4 cup red curry paste (see above)
    1 can (13.5 ounces) unsweetened
        coconut milk
    2 teaspoons salt
    1 tablespoon palm sugar or
        granulated sugar
    1/4 cup fresh lime juice

To make the red curry paste: Remove the stems and seeds from the chiles. Soak them in hot water for 15 minutes. Set them aside. In a dry cast-iron pan, toast the cumin seeds, caraway seeds, peppercorns, and coriander seeds over low heat until fragrant, about 3 minutes. Cool the spices and then grind together with the Kaffir lime leaves in a spice or coffee grinder until very fine.

Drain and chop the chile peppers. In a pan over low heat, sauté the chile peppers, shallots, garlic, ginger, and lemon grass in the vegetable oil until tender, about 5 minutes. Put the vegetables, ground spices, lime peel, and shrimp paste into the bowl of a food processor and process until you have a smooth paste, scraping down the sides once or twice. Stored in a sealed jar in the refrigerator, the paste keeps for about 3 weeks.

Yields 1 cup.

To make the vegetable curry: In a large pot, bring 2 quarts of salted water to a rolling boil. Add the carrots, snow peas, daikon, turnips, and broccoli and blanch for 2 minutes. Remove the vegetables with a slotted spoon, rinse them under cold running water to set the color and set them aside. Bring the water to a boil again and blanch the greens briefly. Drain and rinse them with cold water and set them aside with the other vegetables.

In a large pan, over low heat, sauté the curry paste for 3 minutes. Stir in the coconut milk, salt, palm sugar, and fresh lime juice. Heat the sauce but do not boil or it will curdle. Add the vegetables to the pan, toss together till well combined and adjust the seasoning. Serve over steamed rice.

Serves 4 to 6.

Vegetable Tempura

Tempura is a classic Japanese presentation and when done well is delightfully light and crunchy. Unlike most Japanese dishes, this is a meal that should be served piping hot. Note: I've listed some of my favorite vegetables for tempura. Other vegetables, such as broccoli, yard-long beans, bell peppers, bamboo shoots, daikon radish, and snow peas can also be used.

You will need a heavy deep pot for frying; a slotted spoon for lifting the fried foods out of the oil; a platter lined with paper towels to drain the fried vegetables; and a pair of long, wooden chopsticks (called cooking chopsticks) to dip the vegetables in the batter.

For the batter:

  1 egg yolk

  1 cup ice water

  1 to 1 1/4 cups sifted cake flour

  1 pinch baking soda

For the tempura vegetables:

  1 thin Japanese eggplant, sliced
    1/8 inch thick

  1 carrot, sliced into thin coins on
    the oblique

  1 zucchini, sliced 1/4 inch thick on
    the oblique

  1/2 sweet potato, peeled and sliced
    about 1/8 inch thick

  8 fresh, small button mushrooms

  8 slices of winter squash, peeled
    and sliced about 1/8 inch thick

  Perilla leaves

  Shungiku leaves

For the dipping sauce:

  1 cup dashi (see the recipe on page
    73)

  3 tablespoons soy sauce

  3 tablespoons mirin

  Pinch of salt

For the condiments:

  1/2 cup peeled, grated white daikon
    radish

  2 teaspoons grated fresh ginger
    root

  Lemon wedges

To make the batter: With a fork, combine the egg yolk with the ice water in a small bowl. The batter should be the texture of heavy cream; just thick enough to coat the vegetables. Just before frying the vegetables, stir in the flour and the baking soda, beating just long enough to combine without overworking the batter.

To make the tempura: The key to good tempura is as follows: use only fresh vegetable oil.

The oil should be at least 3 inches deep. The ideal frying temperature for vegetables is 320°F to 340°F. To test, drop a bit of batter into the oil. It should drop to the bottom and then rise slowly to the surface. Be careful not to overheat the oil; if the oil smokes, it is too hot. Do not crowd the pot; for best results less than half the oil surface should be covered with vegetable pieces. Have all your ingredients at hand and arranged in the order that you will use them.

Preheat the oven to warm, about 200°F. To cook, coat each vegetable piece with the batter and fry for one minute. With the chopsticks turn the pieces and fry for another minute until the pieces are golden and puff up. Drain the vegetables on the paper towels and skim crumbs from the oil using a metal slotted spoon. Place the vegetable slices on a warm platter and keep them in the oven until you are done, or better yet, serve each piece to your guests as they come out of the oil. Repeat the process with the other vegetables.

To serve the tempura: Make the sauce by heating the dashi, add then stirring in the soy sauce, mirin, and salt. As is traditionally done in Japan, provide each diner with a shallow bowl of the warm dipping sauce, to which they can add grated daikon and ginger to taste. Serve the tempura accompanied by the lemon wedges.

Serves 4.

appendix A planting and maintenance

This section covers the basics of planning a vegetable garden, preparing the soil, starting seeds, transplanting, fertilizing, mulching, composting, installing irrigation, watering, weeding, crop rotation, and using floating row covers.

Planning Your Vegetable Garden

You can interplant Asian vegetables and herbs among your ornamental flowers—many, such as amaranth and peppers, are quite beautiful—raise them in large containers or planter boxes; or add them to your existing vegetable garden. If you have no vegetable garden, you can design one. The first step in planning any vegetable garden is choosing a suitable site. Most chefs recommend locating the edible garden as close to the kitchen as possible, and I heartily agree. Beyond that, most vegetables need at least six hours of sun (eight is better)—except in warm, humid areas, where afternoon or some filtered shade is best. Most annual vegetables also need fairly rich, well-drained soil with lots of added organic matter.

Take note of what type of soil you have and how well it drains. Annual vegetables need to grow fast and with little stress to be tender and mild. Their roots need air, and if the soil stays waterlogged for long, roots suffocate or are prone to root rot. If you are unsure how well a particular area in your garden drains, dig a hole about 10 inches deep and 10 inches across, where you plan to put your garden, and fill it with water. The next day, fill it again—if it still has water in it 8 to 10 hours later, you need to find another place in the garden that will drain much faster, amend your soil with much organic matter and mound it up at least 6 to 8 inches above the ground level, or grow your vegetables in containers. A sandy soil that drains too fast also calls for the addition of copious amounts of organic matter.

Find out, too, what your soil pH is. Nurseries have kits to test your soil's pH and a university extension service can lead you to sources of soil tests and soil experts. Most vegetables grow best in soil with a pH between 6.0 to 7.0—in other words, slightly acidic. As a rule, rainy climates have acidic soil that needs the pH raised, usually by adding lime, and arid climates have fairly neutral or alkaline soil that needs extra organic matter to lower the pH.

Once you've decided on where you are going to plant, it's time to choose your vegetables. Your major consideration is, of course, what flavors you enjoy using in the kitchen. With this in mind, look for species and varieties that grow well in your climate. As a rule, gardeners in northern climates and high elevations look for vegetables that tolerate cool or short summer conditions. Gardeners in hot, humid areas require plants that tolerate diseases well and must carefully choose heat-tolerant vegetables.

The USDA Plant Hardiness Zone Map has grouped eleven zones according to winter lows, a help in choosing perennial plants but of limited use for annual vegetables. Of more interest to the vegetable gardener is the AHS Plant Heat-Zone Map, published by the American Horticultural Society. The heat map details twelve zones that indicate the average number of days each year when a given area experiences temperatures of 86°F or higher—the temperature at which many plants, including peas and most salad greens, begin to suffer physiological damage. In "The Encyclopedia of Asian Vegetables," I indicate which varieties have a low tolerance to high temperatures and those that grow well in hot weather. See the Bibliography for information on obtaining the heat map.

Crop placement must also be considered. Take care not to plant tall crops, such as cucumbers, on a trellis where they will shade sun-loving plants, such as peppers. Setting out a plan for crop rotation is wise at this point, too. (See the Crop Rotation entry on page 94.)

Other design features to consider include bed size, paths, and fences. A garden of a few hundred square feet, or more, needs a path or two and the soil to be arranged in beds. Paths through any garden should be at least 3 feet across to provide ample room for walking and using a wheelbarrow, and beds should generally be limited to 5 feet across, as that is the average distance a person can reach into the bed to harvest or pull weeds from both sides. Protection, too, is often needed, so consider putting a fence or wall around the garden to give it a stronger design and to keep out rabbits, woodchucks, and the resident dog. Assuming you have chosen a nice, sunny area, selected a design, and determined that your soil drains properly, you are ready to prepare the soil.

Preparing the Soil

To prepare the soil for a new vegetable garden, first remove large rocks and weeds. Dig out any perennial weeds, especially perennial grasses like Bermuda and quack grass. You need to sift and closely examine each shovelful for every little piece of their roots, or they will regrow with a vengeance. If you are taking up part of a lawn, the sod needs to be removed. If it is a small area, this can be done with a flat spade. Removing large sections, though, warrants renting a sod cutter. Next, when the soil is not too wet, spade over the area.

Most vegetables are heavy feeders, and few soils support them without being supplemented with much organic matter and nutrients. The big-three nutrients are nitrogen (N), phosphorus (P), and potassium (K)—the ones most frequently found in fertilizers. Calcium, magnesium, and sulfur are also important plant nutrients, and plants need a number of trace minerals for healthy growth, among them iron, zinc, boron, copper, and manganese. A soil test is the best way to see what your soil needs. In general, most soils benefit from at least an application of an organic nitrogen fertilizer. While it's hard to say what your soil needs without a test, the following gives you a rough idea of how much you need per 100 square feet of average soil.

For nitrogen, apply blood meal at 2 pounds, or fish meal at 2 1/4 pounds; for phosphorus, apply 2 pounds bonemeal; for potassium, apply kelp meal according to the package or, in acidic soils, 1 1/2 pounds of wood ashes. Kelp meal also provides most trace minerals. (The addition of so many nutrients will not be needed in subsequent years if composting and mulching are practiced, especially if you rotate your crops and use cover crops.)

After the area is spaded, cover it with 4 or 5 inches of compost, 1 or 2 inches of well-aged manure, and any other needed fertilizers. Add fertilizers by sprinkling them over the soil. If a soil test indicates that your soil

Raked and graded garden bed ready for planting

is too acidic, lime can be added at this point, though it is best to apply lime in the fall so that it has time to react with the soil before spring planting. Incorporate all the ingredients thoroughly by turning the soil over with a spade, working the amendments into the top 6 to 12 inches. If your garden is large or the soil is very hard to work, you might use a rototiller. (When you put in a garden for the first time, a rototiller can be very helpful. However, research has shown that continued use of tillers is hard on soil structure and quickly burns up valuable organic matter.)

Finally, grade and rake the area. You are now ready to form the beds and paths. Because of all the added materials, the beds are now elevated above the paths-which further helps drainage. Slope the sides of the beds so that loose soil is not easily washed or knocked onto the paths. Some gardeners add a brick or wood edging to outline the beds. Some sort of gravel, brick, stone, or mulch is needed on the paths to forestall weed growth and to prevent your feet from getting wet and muddy.

The last task before planting your garden is providing support for vining crops like yard-long beans and bitter melon. There are many types of supports, from simple stakes to elaborate wire cages; whichever you choose, installing them before you plant is best.

Starting from Seeds

You can grow all annual vegetables from seeds. They can be started indoors in flats or other well-drained containers, outdoors in a cold frame, or, depending on the time of year, directly in the garden. When I start annual vegetables inside, I seed them in either plastic pony packs that I recycle from the nursery or in compartmentalized Styrofoam containers, variously called plugs and speedling trays (available from mail-order garden-supply houses). Whatever type of container you use, the soil depth should be 2 to 3 inches. Any shallower, and the soil dries out too fast, and deeper soil is usually a waste of seed-starting soil and water.

Starting seeds inside gives your seedlings a safe start away from slugs and birds. It also allows gardeners in cold or hot climates to get a jump on the season. Many vegetables can be started 4 to 6 weeks before the last expected frost date and then transplanted out into the garden as soon as the soil can be worked. Furthermore, some vegetables are sensitive to high temperatures; by starting fall crops inside in mid- or late summer, the seeds germinate and the seedlings get a good start and are ready to be transplanted outside in early fall, when the weather starts to cool.

The cultural needs of seeds vary widely among species; still, some basic rules apply to most seeding procedures. First, whether starting seeds in the ground or in a container, make sure you have loose, water-retentive soil that drains well. Good drainage is important because seeds can get waterlogged, and too much water can lead to damping off, a fungal disease that kills seedlings at the soil line. Commercial starting mixes are usually best because they have been sterilized to remove weed seeds; however, the quality varies greatly from brand to brand and I find most lack enough nitrogen, so I water with a weak solution of fish emulsion when I plant the seeds, and again a week or so later.

Smooth the soil surface and plant the seeds at the recommended depth. Information on seed depth is included in "The Encyclopedia of Asian Vegetables" as well as on the back of most seed packages.

Pat down the seeds and water carefully to make the seed bed moist but not soggy. Mark the name of the plant and variety and the date of seeding on a plastic or wooden label and place it at the head of the row. When starting seeds outside, protect the seed bed with either floating row covers or bird netting to keep out critters. If slugs and snails are a problem, circle the area with hardwood ashes or diatomaceous earth to keep them away and go out at night with a flashlight to catch any that cross the barrier. If you start seeds in containers, put the seedling tray in a warm, but not hot, place to help seeds germinate more quickly.

When starting seeds inside, once they have germinated, it's imperative that they immediately be given a high-quality source of light; otherwise, the new seedlings will be spindly and pale. A greenhouse, sun-porch, or south-facing window with no overhang will suffice, provided it is warm. If such a place is not available, use fluorescent lights, which are available from home-supply stores and specialty mail-order houses. The lights are hung just above the plants for maximum light (no farther than 3 or 4 inches away, at most) and moved up as the plants get taller. Another option I use if the weather is above 60°F is to put my seedling trays outside on a table in the sun and protect them with bird netting during the day, bringing them in at night.

Once seedlings are up, keep them moist and, if you seeded thickly and have crowded plants, thin some out. It's less damaging to do so with small scissors. Cut the little plants out, leaving the remaining seedlings an inch or so apart. Do not transplant your seedlings until they have their second set of true leaves (the first leaves that sprout from a seed are called seed leaves and usually look different from the later true leaves). If the seedlings are tender, wait until all danger of frost is past before you set them out. In fact, don't put out heat-loving melons and peppers until the weather is thoroughly warmed up and stable. Young plants started indoors should be hardened off before they are planted in the garden—that is, they should be put outside in a sheltered place for a few days in their containers to let them get used to the differences in temperature, humidity, and air movement outside. A cold frame is perfect for hardening off plants.

Transplanting

Before setting transplants out in the garden, check to see if a mat of roots has formed at the bottom of the root ball. Open it up so the roots won't continue to grow in a tangled mass. I set the plant in the ground at the same height as it was in the container, pat the plant in place gently by hand, and water in each plant well to remove air bubbles. I space plants so that they won't be crowded once they mature; when vegetables grow too close together, they become prone to rot diseases and mildew. If I'm planting on a very hot day or the transplants have been in a protected greenhouse, I shade them by placing a shingle or such on the sunny side of the plants. I then install my irrigation ooze tubing (see Watering and Irrigation Systems, page 93) and mulch with a few inches of organic matter. I keep the transplants moist but not soggy for the first few weeks.

Mulching

Mulching reduces moisture loss, prevents erosion, controls weeds, and minimizes soil compaction. When the mulch is an organic material, it adds nutrients and organic matter to the soil as it decomposes, making heavy clay more porous and helping sandy soil retain moisture. Organic mulches include finished compost from your compost pile, grass clippings, pine needles, composted sawdust, straw, and the many agricultural byproducts like rice hulls and apple and grape pomace. Layers of black-and-white newspaper are particularly good at deterring weeds. Coarse, woody mulches,

Mulch using black plastic

such as wood and bark chips and shredded bark, do not work well as mulches in vegetable gardens, as they break down slowly and take nitrogen from the soil. However, they do make good mulches for pathways and other areas of a more permanent nature.

Among the many benefits of mulching is the moderation of soil temperatures. A thick organic mulch helps keep roots from getting too hot in hot summer regions and a black plastic mulch warms soil in cool regions in preparation for spring transplanting. A variation on black plastic, in red and green, called IRT (Infra-Red Transmitting) is on the market. It has the heat-transmitting qualities of clear plastic—in other words, it warms soil even more than regular black plastic and also discourages weed growth (which clear plastic does not). The red and green IRT is available from garden supply stores and mail-order garden-suppliers. When you remove the plastic mulches, dispose of them. These plastics don't decompose, although there are some brands that claim to; it is more likely that they degrade into small pieces.

Composting

Compost is the humus-rich result of the decomposition of organic matter, such as leaves and garden trimmings. The objective of maintaining a composting system is to speed up decomposition and centralize the material so you can gather it up and spread it where it will do the most good. Compost's benefits include providing nutrients to plants in a slow-release, balanced fashion; helping break up clay soil; aiding sandy soil to retain moisture; and correcting pH problems. On top of that, compost is free, it can be made at home, and it is an excellent way to recycle yard and kitchen wastes. Compost can be used as a soil additive or a mulch.

There need be no great mystique about composting. To create the environment needed by the decay-causing microorganisms that do all the work, just include the following four ingredients, mixed well: 3 or 4 parts brown material high in carbon, such as dry leaves, dry grass, and even shredded black-and-white newspaper; one part green material high in nitrogen, such as fresh grass clippings, fresh garden trimmings,

A three-bin composting system

barnyard manure, and kitchen trimmings like pea pods and carrot tops; water in moderate amounts, so that the mixture is moist but not soggy; and air to supply oxygen to the microorganisms. Bury the kitchen trimmings within the pile so as not to attract flies. Cut up any large pieces of material. Exclude weeds that have gone to seed and noxious perennial weeds such as Bermuda grass, because they can lead to the growth of those weeds in the garden. Do not add meat, fat, diseased plants of any kind, woody branches, or cat or dog manure.

I don't stress myself about the proper proportions of compost materials, as long as I have a fairly good mix of materials from the garden. If the decomposition is too slow, it is usually because the pile has too much brown material, is too dry, or needs air. If the pile smells, there is too much green material or it is too wet. To speed decomposition, I often chop or shred the materials before adding them to the pile and I may turn the pile occasionally to get additional oxygen to all parts. During decomposition, the materials can become quite hot and steamy, which is good; however, it is not mandatory that the compost become extremely hot.

You can make compost in a simple pile, in wire or wood bins, or in rather expensive containers. The size should be about 3 feet high, wide, and deep (3 cubic feet) for the most efficient decomposition and so the

pile is easily workable. It can be larger, but too much so and it becomes hard to manage. In a rainy climate, it's a good idea to have a cover for the compost. I like to use three bins. I collect the compost materials in one bin, have a working bin, and when that bin is full, I turn the contents into the last bin, where it finishes its decomposition. I sift the finished compost into empty garbage cans so it does not leach its nutrients into the soil. The empty bin is then ready to fill again.

Watering and Irrigation Systems

There is no easy formula for determining the correct amount or frequency of watering. Proper watering takes experience and observation. In addition to the specific watering needs of individual plants, the amount of watering required depends on soil type, wind conditions, and air temperature. To water properly, you must learn how to recognize water-stress symptoms (often a dulling of foliage color as well as the better-known symptoms of drooping leaves and wilting), how much to water (too much is as bad as too little), and how to water. Some general rules are:

1. Water deeply. Except for seed beds, most plants need infrequent deep watering rather than frequent light sprinkling.

2. To ensure proper absorption, apply water at a rate slow enough to prevent runoff.

3. Do not use overhead watering systems when the wind is blowing.

4. Try to water in the morning so that foliage has time to dry off before nightfall, thus preventing some disease problems. In addition, because of the cooler temperature, less water is lost to evaporation.

5. Test your watering system occasionally to make sure it covers the area evenly.

6. Use methods and tools that conserve water. When using a hose, use a nozzle or watering wand that shuts off the water while you move from one container or planting bed to another. Soaker hoses, made of canvas or recycled tires, and other ooze and drip-irrigation systems apply water slowly and use water more efficiently than do overhead systems.

Drip- or the related ooze- and trickle irrigation systems are advisable wherever feasible, and most gardens are well suited to them. Drip systems deliver water one drop at a time through spaghetti-like emitter tubes or plastic pipe with emitters that drip water right onto the root zone of each plant. Because of the time and effort involved in installing one or two emitters per plant, drip systems work best for permanent plantings. The lines require continual maintenance to make sure the individual emitters are not clogged.

Similar systems, called ooze systems, deliver water through holes made every 6 or 12 inches along solid flexible tubing or ooze along an entirely porous hose. Both of these systems work well in vegetable gardens. Neither system is as prone to clogging as are drip emitters. The solid type is made of plastic and is often called laser tubing. It is pressure compensated, which means the flow of water is even throughout the length of the tubing. The high-quality brands have a built-in mechanism to minimize clogging and are made of tubing that will not expand in hot weather and, consequently, pop off its fittings. (Some of the inexpensive drip-irrigation kits can make you crazy!)

The porous hose types are made from recycled tires and come in two sizes—a standard hose diameter of 1 inch, great for shrubs and trees planted in a row, and $1/4$-inch tubing that can be snaked around beds of small plants. Neither are pressure compensated, which means the plants nearest the source of water get more water than those at the end of the line. It also means they do not work well if there is any slope.

All types of drip emitter and ooze systems are installed after the plants or seeds are in the ground and are held in place with ground staples. To install any such system, you must also install an antisiphon valve at the water source to prevent dirty garden water from being drawn up into the house's drinking water. Further, a filter is needed to prevent debris from clogging the emitters. To set up the system, 1-inch distribution tubing is connected to the water source and laid out around the perimeter of the garden. Then smaller-diameter drip and ooze lines are connected to this. As you can see, installing these systems requires some thought and time.

You can order these systems from specialty mail-order garden and irrigation sources or by visiting your local plumbing-supply store. I find the latter to be the best solution for all my irrigation problems. Over the years, I've found that plumbing-supply stores offer professional-quality supplies, usually for less money than the so-called inexpensive kits available in home-supply stores and some nurseries. In addition to excellent materials, the professionals there help you to lay out an irrigation design tailored to your garden. Whether you choose an emitter or an ooze system, when you go to buy your tubing, be prepared by bringing a rough drawing of the area to be irrigated—with dimensions, the location of the water source and any slopes, and, if possible, the water pressure at your water source. Let the professionals walk you through the steps and help pick out supplies that best fit your site.

Problems aside, all forms of drip and ooze irrigation are more efficient than furrow or standard overhead watering with respect to delivering water to its precise destination; they are well worth considering. They deliver water slowly, so it doesn't run off. They also water deeply, which encourages deep rooting. They also eliminate many disease problems, and because so little of the soil surface is moist, there are fewer

weeds. Finally, they have the potential to waste a lot less water.

Weeding

Weeding is needed to make sure unwanted plants don't compete with and overpower your vegetables and herbs. A small triangular hoe will help you weed a small garden if you start when the weeds are young and easily hoed. If you allow the weeds to get large, a session of hand pulling is needed. Be cautious, as many plants are shallow rooted. Applying a mulch is a great way to cut down on weeds; however, if you have a big problem with slugs in your garden, the mulch gives them more places to hide. Another means of controlling weeds, especially annual weeds like crabgrass and pigweed, is a new organic preemergence herbicide made from corn gluten called Concern Weed Prevention Plus. This gluten meal inhibits the tiny feeder roots of germinating weed seeds so they wither and die. It does not kill existing weeds. Obviously, if you use it among new seedlings or in seed beds, it kills the vegetables too, so it is only useful in areas away from very young plants.

Crop Rotation

Rotating crops in an edible garden has been practiced for centuries. The object is to avoid growing members of the same family in the same spot year after year, as plants in the same family are often prone to the same diseases and pests and deplete the same nutrients. For example, peppers should not follow eggplants or tomatoes, as all are Solanaceae-family plants and all are prone to fusarium wilt. On the other hand, in southeastern gardens, quick-growing cabbage-family plants, such as mustard, make a great crop to rotate with peppers as they discourage the root knot nematodes to which many peppers are susceptible.

Crop rotation is also practiced to help maintain the soil nutrient level. The pea family (legumes), which includes not only peas and beans but also clovers and alfalfa, adds nitrogen to the soil. In contrast, most members of the cabbage, cucumber, and tomato families deplete the soil of nitrogen. Because most vegetables deplete the soil,

knowledgeable gardeners not only rotate their beds with vegetables from different families, they also include an occasional cover crop of clover or alfalfa (or other legume) and other soil benefactors, such as buckwheat. After growing for a few months, these crops are turned under, providing organic matter and many nutrients. Some cover crops (like rye) are grown over the winter to control soil erosion. The seeds of all sorts of cover crops are available from farm suppliers and specialty seed companies.

The following is a short list of related vegetables and herbs. The plants listed for each family are not comprehensive; they are examples of the plants in that family.

Apiaceae (parsley and carrot family)—includes carrots, celeriac, celery, chervil, coriander (cilantro), dill, fennel, lovage, parsley, parsnips

Asteraceae (sunflower and daisy family, also called composites)—includes artichokes, calendulas, celtuce, chicories, dandelions, endives, lettuces, marigolds, tarragon

Brassicaceae (mustard and cabbage family)—includes arugula, broccoli, cabbages, cauliflower, collards, cresses, kale, kohlrabi, komatsuna, mizuna, mustards, radishes, turnips

Chenopodiaceae (goosefoot family)—includes beets, chard, orach, spinach

Cucurbitaceae (cucumber or gourd family)—includes cucumbers, gourds, melons, summer squash, winter squash, pumpkins

Fabaceae (pea family, also called legumes)—includes beans, cowpeas, fava beans, lima beans, peanuts, peas, runner beans, soybeans, sugar peas

Lamiaceae (mint family)—includes basil, mints, oregano, rosemary, sages, summer savory, thymes

Liliaceae (lily family)—includes asparagus, chives, garlic, leeks, onions, Oriental chives, shallots

Solanaceae (nightshade and tomato family)—includes eggplants, peppers, potatoes, tomatillos, tomatoes

Floating row cover

Floating Row Covers

Among the most valuable tools for plant protection in the vegetable garden are floating row covers made of lightweight spunbond polyester or polypropylene fabric. They are laid directly over the plants, where they "float" in place, though they can also be stretched over hoops. These covers can be used to protect plants against cold weather and to shade them in extremely hot and sunny climates.

If used correctly, row covers are a most effective pest control for various beetles and caterpillars, leafhoppers, aphids, and leaf miners. The most lightweight covers, usually called summerweight or insect barriers because they generate little heat buildup, can be used throughout the season for insect control in all but the hottest and coldest climates. They cut down on 10 percent of the sunlight, which is seldom a problem, unless your garden is already partly shady. Heavier versions, sometimes called garden covers under trade names including Reemay and Tufbell, variously cut down from 15 percent to 50 percent of the sunlight—which could be a problem for some plants, such as peppers—but they also raise the temperature underneath from 2°F to 7°F, which can help to protect plants from early fall frosts and to extend the season in

cool-summer areas. Another way to raise the temperature is to use two layers of the lightweight cover.

Other advantages to using floating row covers include:

* The stronger ones protect plants from most songbirds, though not from crafty squirrels and blue jays.

* They raise the humidity around plants, a bonus in arid climates but a problem in humid climates.

* They protect young seedlings from sunburn in summer and in high-altitude gardens.

There are a few limitations to consider:

* These covers keep out pollinating bees needed to produce squash and cucumbers.

* Many of the fabrics last only a year and then start to deteriorate. (I use tattered small pieces to cover containers, in the bottoms of containers to keep out slugs, etc.)

* Row covers use petroleum products and eventually end up in the landfill.

* In very windy areas, tunnels and floating row covers are apt to be blown away or become shredded.

* The heavyweight versions may cut down on too much light and are useful only to help raise temperatures when frost threatens.

Rolls of the fabric, from 5 to 10 feet wide and up to 100 feet long, can be purchased from local nurseries or ordered from garden-supply catalogs. As a rule, mail-order sources offer a wider selection of materials and sizes.

Before you apply your row cover for pest protection, fully prepare the bed and make sure it's free of eggs, larvae, and adult pests. Then install drip irrigation, if you are using it, plant your crop, and mulch (if appropriate). There are two ways to lay a row cover: directly on the plants or stretched over wire hoops. Laying the cover directly on the plants is the easier approach. However, laying it over hoops makes it easier to check underneath. Also, some plants are sensitive to abrasion; if the wind whips the cover around, the tips of the plants may turn brown. When you lay the fiber directly on the plants, leave some slack so plants have room to grow. For both methods, secure the edges completely with bricks, rocks, old pieces of lumber, bent wire hangers, or the U-shaped metal pins sold for this purpose.

To avoid pitfalls, it's critical to check under the row covers from time to time. Check soil moisture, the fibers sometimes shed rain and overhead irrigation water. Check as well for weeds; the protective fiber aids their growth too. Most important, check for insect pests that may be trapped inside.

appendix B
pest and
disease
control

The following sections cover a large number of pests and diseases. An individual gardener, however, will encounter few such problems in a lifetime of gardening. Good garden planning, good hygiene, and an awareness of major symptoms will keep problems to a minimum and give you many hours to enjoy your garden and feast on its bounty.

Some spoilers, though, may need control. For years, controls were presented as a list of critters and diseases, followed by the newest and best chemical to control them. But times have changed, and we now know that chasing the latest chemical to fortify our arsenal is a bit like chasing our tail. That's because most pesticides, both insecticides and fungicides, kill beneficial insects as well as the pests; therefore, the more we spray, the more we are forced to spray. Nowadays, we've learned that successful pest control focuses on prevention, plus beefing up the natural ecosystem so beneficial insects are on pest patrol. How does that translate to pest control for the vegetable garden directly?

1. When possible, seek varieties resistant to pests and diseases.

2. Use mechanical means to prevent insect pests from damaging plants. For example, cover young cabbage-family plants with floating row covers to keep away flea beetles and imported cabbageworm; sprinkle wood ashes around plants to prevent cabbage root maggot and slug damage; and put cardboard collars around young pepper, cabbage, and cucumber seedlings to prevent cutworms from destroying them.

3. Clean up diseased foliage and dispose of it in the garbage to cut down on the cycle of infection.

4. Rotate your crops so that plants from the same family are not planted in the same place for two consecutive seasons. (See Crop Rotation, page 94.)

5. Encourage and provide food for beneficial insects. In the vegetable garden, this translates to letting a few selected vegetables go to flower and growing flowering herbs and ornamentals to provide a season-long source of nectar and pollen for beneficial insects.

Beneficial Insects

In a nutshell, few insects are potential problems; most are either neutral or beneficial to the gardener. Given the chance, the beneficial insects do much of your insect control for you, provided that you don't use pesticides, which are apt to kill them as well as the problem insects. Like predatory lions stalking zebra, predatory ladybugs (lady beetles) and lacewing larvae hunt and eat aphids that might be attracted to your Chinese cabbage. Or say a mini-wasp parasitoid lays eggs in the aphids. If you spray those aphids, even with a so-called benign pesticide such as insecticidal soap or pyrethrum, you'll kill off those ladybugs and lacewings and that baby parasitoid wasp too. Most insecticides are broad spectrum, which means that they kill insects indiscriminately, not just the pests. In my opinion, organic gardeners who regularly use organic broad-spectrum insecticides have missed this point. While it is true they are using an "organic" pesticide, they may actually be eliminating a truly organic means of control, the beneficial insects.

Unfortunately, many gardeners are not aware of the benefits of the predator-prey relationship and are not able to recognize beneficial insects. The following sections will help you to identify both helpful and pest organisms. A more detailed aid for identifying insects is *Rodale's Color Handbook of Garden Insects,* by Anna Carr. A hand lens is an invaluable and inexpensive tool that will also help you to identify the insects in your garden.

Predators and Parasitoids

Insects that feed on other insects are divided into two types, the predators and the parasitoids. Predators are mobile. They stalk plants looking for such plant feeders as aphids and mites. Parasitoids, on the other hand, are insects that develop in or on the bodies, pupae, or eggs of host insects. Most parasitoids are minute wasps or flies whose larvae (young stages) eat other insects from within. Some of the wasps are so small they can develop within an aphid or an insect egg. One parasitoid egg can divide into several identical cells, each developing into identical mini-wasp larvae, which then can kill an entire caterpillar. Though nearly invisible to most gardeners, parasitoids are the most specific and effective means of insect control.

The predator-prey relationship can be a fairly stable situation; when the natural system is working properly, pest insects inhabiting the garden along with the predators and parasitoids seldom become a problem. Sometimes, though, the system breaks down. For example, a number of imported pests have taken hold in this country and unfortunately, when they were brought here, their natural predators did not accompany them. Four pesky examples are Japanese beetles, the European brown snail, the white cabbage butterfly, and flea beetles. None of these organisms has natural enemies in this country that provide sufficient controls. Where they occur, it is sometimes necessary to use physical means or selective pesticides that kill only the problem insect.

Weather extremes sometime produce imbalances as well. For example, long stretches of hot, dry weather favor grasshoppers that invade vegetable gardens, because the diseases that keep them in check are more prevalent under moist conditions. Predator-prey relationships also get out of balance because gardening practices often inadvertently work in favor of the pests. When gardeners spray with broad-spectrum pesticides regularly, for example, not all the insects in the garden are killed—and as predators and parasitoids generally reproduce more slowly than do the pests, regular spraying usually tips the balance in favor of the pests. Further, all too often the average yard has few plants that produce nectar for beneficial insects; instead it is filled with grass and shrubs, so that when a few vegetables are put in, the new plants attract the aphids but not the beneficials. Being aware of the effect of these practices will help you to create a vegetable garden that is relatively free of many pest problems.

Attracting Beneficial Insects

Besides reducing your use of pesticides, the key to keeping a healthy balance in your garden is providing a diversity of plants, including plenty that produce nectar and pollen. Nectar is the primary food of the adult stage and some larval stages of many beneficial insects. Interplanting your vegetables with flowers and numerous herbs helps to attract them. Ornamentals, like species zinnias, marigolds, alyssum, and yarrow, provide many flowers over a long season and are shallow enough for insects to reach the nectar. Large, dense flowers like tea roses and dahlias are useless, as their nectar is out of reach. A number of the herbs are rich nectar sources, including fennel, dill, anise, chervil, oregano, thyme, and parsley. Allowing a few of your vegetables, like carrots, coriander, and mustards, go to flower is helpful because their tiny flowers, full of nectar and pollen, are just what many of the beneficial insects need.

Following are a few of the predatory and parasitoid insects helpful in the garden. Their preservation and protection should be a major goal of your pest-control strategy.

Ground beetles and their larvae are all predators. Most adult ground beetles are fairly large black beetles that scurry out from under plants and containers when you disturb them. Their favorite foods are soft-bodied larvae like cutworms and root maggots (root maggots eat cabbage-family plants); some ground beetles even eat snails and slugs. If supplied with an undisturbed place to live, like your compost area or groupings of perennial plantings, ground beetles will be consistent residents of your garden.

Lacewings are one of the most effective insect predators in the home garden. They are small green or brown gossamer-winged insects that, in their adult stage, eat flower nectar, pollen, aphid honeydew, and sometimes aphids and mealybugs. In the larval stage, they look like little tan alligators. Called aphid lions, the larvae are fierce predators of aphids, mites, and whiteflies—all occasional pests that suck plant sap. If you are having problems with sucking insects in your garden, consider purchasing lacewing eggs or larvae by mail order to jump-start your lacewing population. Remember to plant lots of nectar plants to keep the population going from year to year.

Lady beetles (ladybugs) are the best known of the beneficial garden insects. Actually, there are about 400 species of lady beetles in North America alone. They come in a variety of colors and markings in addition to the familiar red with black spots, but they are never green. Lady beetles and their fierce-looking alligator-shaped larvae eat copious amounts of aphids and other small insects.

Spiders are close relatives of insects. There are hundreds of species, and they are some of the most effective predators of a great range of pest insects.

Syrphid flies (also called flowerflies and hover flies) look like very small bees hovering over flowers, but they have only two wings. Many have yellow and black stripes on their body. Their larvae are small green maggots that inhabit leaves and eat aphids, other small sucking insects, and mites.

Wasps comprise a large family of insects with transparent wings. Unfortunately, the few large wasps that sting have given wasps a bad name. In fact, all wasps are either insect predators or parasitoids. The mini-wasps are usually parasitoids, and the adult female lays her eggs in such insects as aphids, whitefly larvae, and caterpillars—and the developing wasp larvae devour the host. These miniature wasps are also available for purchase from insectaries and are especially effective when released in greenhouses.

Pests

The following pests are sometimes a problem in the vegetable garden.

Aphids are soft-bodied, small green, black, pink, or gray insects that produce many generations in one season. They suck plant juices and exude honeydew. Sometimes leaves under the aphids turn black from a mold growing on the nutrient-rich honeydew. Aphids are particularly attracted to cabbage-family plants, beans, and peas. Aphid populations can build up, especially in the spring, before beneficial insects are present in large numbers and when plants are covered by row covers or are growing in cold frames. The presence of aphids sometimes indicates that the plant is under stress—perhaps the cabbage isn't getting enough water and sunlight. Check first to see if stress is a problem and then try to correct it. Look also for aphid mummies and other natural enemies mentioned previously. Mummies are swollen brown or metallic-looking aphids. Inside the mummy, a wasp parasitoid is growing. They are valuable, so keep them. To remove aphids generally, wash the foliage with a strong blast of water and cut back the foliage if the aphids persist. Fertilize and water the plant and check on it in a few days. Repeat with the water spray a few more times. In extreme situations, spray with insecticidal soap or a neem product.

A number of **beetles** are garden pests. They include Mexican bean beetles, cucumber beetles, flea beetles, and wireworms (the larvae of click beetles). All are a problem throughout most of North America. Colorado potato beetles and Japanese beetles are primarily a problem in the eastern United States. Mexican bean beetles look like brown lady beetles with oval black spots; as their name implies, they feed on beans. Cucumber beetles are ladybuglike green or yellow green beetles with either black stripes or black spots. Their larvae feed on the roots of corn and other vegetables. The adults devour members of the cucumber family, corn tassels, beans, and some salad greens. Flea beetles are minuscule black-and-white striped beetles hardly big enough to be seen. The grubs feed on the roots and lower leaves of many vegetables, and the adults chew on the leaves of eggplants, radishes, peppers, and other plants, causing the leaves to look shot full of tiny holes. The adult click beetle is rarely seen, and its young, brown, $1^{1}/_{2}$-inch-long shiny larva called a wireworm, works underground and damages tubers, seeds, and roots. Colorado potato beetles are larger and rounder than lady beetles and have red brown heads and black and yellow striped backs. Adults and larvae eat the leaves of eggplants and peppers as well as other plants in the Solanaceae family, so crop rotation with another plant family is essential if these beetles are a problem in your area. Japanese beetles are fairly large metallic blue or green beetles with coppery wings. The larval stage (a white grub) lives on the roots of grasses, and the adult skeletonizes leaves and chews flowers and buds of beans and many other plants.

The larger beetles, if not in great numbers, can be controlled by hand picking—in the morning is best, when the beetles are slower. Knock them into a bowl or bucket of soapy water. Flea beetles are too small to gather by hand; try a handheld vacuum instead. Insecticidal soap on the underside of the leaves is also effective on flea beetles. Wireworms can be trapped by putting cut pieces of potato or carrot every 5 feet or so in the soil and then digging them up after a few days. Destroy the worms.

Because many beetle species winter over in the soil, crop rotation and fall cleanup is vital. Polyester row covers securely fastened to the ground can provide excellent control for most beetles, if used in combination with crop rotation. Obviously, row covers are of no use if the beetles are in a larval stage and ready to emerge from the soil under the row cover or if the adults are already established on the plant. Row covers also have limited use on plants (such as cucumbers and winter melons) that need bees to pollinate the blooms, as bees also are excluded.

New evidence indicates that beneficial nematodes are effective in controlling most pest beetles if applied during the beetles' soil-dwelling larval stage. Colorado potato beetles can also be controlled, when very young, by applications of *Bacillus thuringiensis* var. *san diego,* a beetle Bt that has proven effective for flea beetles, as well. Azadirachtin (the active ingredient in some formulations of neem) is also effective against the immature stage of most beetles and can act as a feeding deterrent for adults. Japanese beetle populations can also be reduced by applications of milkyspore, a naturally occurring soil-borne disease that infects the beetle in its grub stage—though the disease is slow to work. The grubs primarily feed in lawns; the application of lime, if your lawn is acidic, is reported to help control grubs, too.

Caterpillars (sometimes called loopers and worms) are the immature stage of moths and butterflies. Most pose no problem in our gardens and we encourage them to visit, but a few are a problem in the vegetable garden. Among the most notorious are the beanloopers, cutworms, and the numerous cabbage worms and loopers that chew ragged holes in leaves. Natural controls include birds, wasps, and disease. Encourage birds by providing a birdbath, shelter, and berry-producing shrubs. Tolerate wasp nests, if they're not a threat, and provide nectar plants for the miniwasps. Hand picking is very effective as well. The disease *Bacillus thuringiensis* var. *kurstaki* is available as a spray in a number of formulations. Brands include Bt kurstaki, Dipel, and Thuricide. It is a bacteria that, if applied when the caterpillar is fairly young, causes it to starve to death. Bt-k Bait contains the disease and lures budworms away from vegetables and to it. I seldom use Bt in any form, as it also kills all butterfly and harmless moth larvae.

Cutworms are the caterpillar stage of various moth species. They are usually found in the soil and curl up into a ball when disturbed. Cutworms are a particular problem on annual vegetables when the seedlings first appear and when young transplants are set out. The cutworm often chews off the stem right at the soil line, killing the plant. Control cutworms by using cardboard collars or bottomless tin cans around the plant stem; be sure to sink these collars 1 inch into the ground. *Bacillus* *thuringiensis* gives limited control. Trichogramma mini-wasps and black ground beetles are among cutworms' natural enemies, but they are often not present in a new garden.

Leaf miners tunnel through leaves, disfiguring them by causing patches of dead tissue where they feed; they do not burrow into the roots. Leaf miners are the larvae of a small fly and can be controlled somewhat by neem or by applying beneficial nematodes.

Mites are among the few arachnids (spiders and their kin) that pose a problem. Mites are so small that a hand lens is usually needed to see them. They become a problem when they reproduce in great numbers. A symptom of serious mite damage is stippling on the leaves in the form of tiny white or yellow spots, sometimes accompanied by tiny webs. The major natural predators of pest mites are predatory mites, mite-eating thrips, and syrphid flies.

Mites are most likely to thrive on dusty leaves and in warm weather. A routine foliage wash and misting of sensitive vegetables helps control mites. Mites are seldom a serious problem unless heavy-duty pesticides that kill off predatory mites are used or plants are grown in the house. Cut back the plants and, if you're using heavy-duty pesticides, stop the applications, and the balance could return. If all else fails, use the neem derivative Green Light Fruit, Nut, and Vegetable Spray or dispose of the plant.

Nematodes are microscopic round worms that inhabit the soil in most of the United States, particularly in the Southeast. Most nematode species live on decaying matter or are predatory on other nematodes, insects, or bacteria. A few types are parasitic, attaching themselves to the roots of plants. Edible plants particularly susceptible to nematode damage include beans, melons, peppers, eggplants, and some perennial herbs. The symptoms of nematode damage are stunted-looking plants and small swellings or lesions on the roots.

Rotate annual vegetables with less susceptible varieties; plant contaminated beds with a blanket of marigolds for a whole season; keep your soil high in organic matter (to encourage fungi and predatory nematodes, both of which act as biological controls); or, if all else fails, grow edibles in containers with sterilized soil.

Snails and slugs are not insects, of course, but mollusks. They are especially fond of greens and seedlings of most vegetables. They feed at night and can go dormant for months in times of stress. In the absence of effective natural enemies (a few snail eggs are consumed by predatory beetles and earwigs), several snail-control strategies can be recommended. As snails and slugs are most active after rain or irrigation, go out and destroy them on such nights. Only repeated forays provide adequate control. Hardwood ashes dusted around susceptible plants gives some control. Planter boxes with a strip of copper applied along the top perimeter boards effectively keep slugs and snails out; they won't cross the barrier. A word of warning: Overhanging leaves that can provide a bridge into the bed will defeat the barrier. Two new organic slug and snail baits, Sluggo and Escar Go!, show promise. They are chelated iron in bait form, which cause the snails and slugs that consume the bait to stop eating and eventually die. There is some question as to whether the iron will build up in the soil and be a problem. As with any bait or pesticide, it is best not to use these regularly or as your only control.

Thrips are tiny, hard-to-see, torpedo-shaped insects that can be a problem on many plants, including peas and onions. The damage they do can be quite noticeable. Leaf-feeding thrips leave a silvery sheen and flecks of discoloration on the leaf surface. To control, keep plants adequately watered, as the predators of thrips live in the moist soil around the plants. If necessary, spot-treat infected plants with insecticidal soap.

Whiteflies are sometimes a problem in mild-winter areas of the country as well as in greenhouses nationwide, especially on eggplants and cucumbers. Whiteflies can be a persistent problem if plants are against a building or fence, where air circulation is limited. In the garden, Encarsia wasps and other parasitoids usually provide adequate whitefly control. Occasionally, especially in cool weather or in greenhouses, whitefly populations may begin to cause serious plant damage (wilting and slowed growth or flowering). Look under the leaves to determine whether the scalelike immobile larvae, the young crawling stage, or the pupae are present in large numbers. If so, wash them off with water from your hose. Repeat the washing 3 days in a row. In addition, try vacuuming the adults with a handheld vacuum early in the day while the weather is still cool and they are less active. Insecticidal soap sprays can be quite effective as well.

Wildlife Problems

Rabbits and mice can cause problems for gardeners. To keep them out, use fine-weave fencing around the vegetable garden. If gophers or moles are a problem, plant large vegetables such as peppers in chicken-wire baskets in the ground. Make the wire stick up 1 foot from the ground so the critters can't reach inside. In severe situations, you might have to line whole beds with chicken wire. Gophers usually need to be trapped. Trapping for moles is less successful, but repellents like MoleMed sometimes help. Cats help with all rodent problems but seldom provide adequate control. Small, portable electric fences help keep raccoons, squirrels, and woodchucks out of the garden. Small-diameter wire mesh, bent into boxes and anchored with ground staples, protects seedlings from squirrels and chipmunks.

Deer are a serious problem—they love vegetables. I've tried myriad repellents, but they gave only short-term control. In some areas, deer cause such severe problems that edible plants can't be grown without tall electric or 9-foot fences and an aggressive dog. The exception is herbs; deer don't feed on most culinary herbs.

Songbirds, starlings, and crows can be major pests of young seedlings, particularly corn and peas. Cover the emerging plants with bird netting and firmly anchor it to the ground so birds can't get under it and feast.

Pest Controls

Insecticidal soap sprays are effective against many pest insects, including caterpillars, aphids, mites, and whiteflies. They can be purchased, or you can make a soap spray at home. As a rule, I recommend purchasing insecticidal soaps, as they are carefully formulated to give the most effective control and are less apt to burn your vegetables. If you do make your own, use a mild liquid dishwashing soap; not caustic detergents.

Neem-based pesticide and fungicide products, which are derived from the neem tree (*Azadirachta indica*), have relatively low toxicity to mammals but are effective against a wide range of insects. Neem products are considered organic pesticides by some organizations but not by others. Products containing azadirachtin, a derivative of neem, are effective because azadirachtin is an insect-growth regulator that affects the ability of immature stages of insects such as leaf miners, cucumber beetles, and aphids to develop to adulthood. BioNeem and Azatin are commercial pesticides containing azadirachtin. Another neem product, Green Light Fruit, Nut, and Vegetable Spray, contains clarified hydrophobic extract of neem oil and is effective against mites, aphids, and some fungus diseases. Neem products are still fairly new in the United States. Although neem was at first thought to be harmless to beneficial insects, some studies now show that some parasitoid beneficial insects that feed on neem-treated pest insects are unable to survive to adulthood.

Pyrethrum, a botanical insecticide, is toxic to a wide range of insects but has relatively low toxicity to most mammals and breaks down quickly. The active ingredients in pyrethrum are pyrethins, derived from chrysanthemum flowers. Do not confuse pyrethrum with pyrethoids, which are much more toxic synthetics that do not biodegrade as quickly. Many pyrethrums have a synergist, piperonyl butoxide (PBO), added to increase the effectiveness. As there is evidence that PBO may affect the human nervous system; try to use pyrethrums without PBO added. Wear gloves, goggles, and a respirator when using any pyrethrum.

Diseases and Deficiencies

Plant diseases are potentially far more damaging to your vegetables than are most insects. There are two types of diseases: those caused by nutrient deficiencies and those caused by pathogens. Diseases caused by pathogens, such as root rots, are difficult to control once they begin. Therefore, most plant-disease-control strategies emphasize prevention rather than cure.

To keep diseases under control, it is very important to plant the right plant in the right place. For instance, phytophthora can be a problem for soybeans if they are planted in poorly drained soil. Check the cultural needs of a plant before placing it in your garden. Proper light, air circulation, temperature, fertilization, and moisture are important factors in disease control. Whenever possible, choose disease-resistant varieties when a particular pathogen is present or when conditions are optimal for the disease. The entries for individual plants in "The Encyclopedia of Asian Vegetables" give specific cultural and variety information. Note that plants infected with disease pathogens should always be discarded, not composted.

Nutritional Deficiencies

For more basic information on plant nutrients, see the soil-preparation information given in Appendix A (page 90). As with pathogens, the best way to solve nutritional problems is to prevent them. While mineral deficiencies affecting vegetables are most often caused by a soil pH below 6 or above 7.5, the most common nutritional deficiency is a lack of nitrogen. Vegetables need fairly high amounts of nitrogen in the soil to keep growing vigorously. Nitrogen deficiency is especially prevalent in sandy soil and in soil low in organic matter. The main symptom of nitrogen deficiency is a pale and slightly yellow cast to the foliage, especially the lower, older leaves. To correct the problem, supplement your beds with a good source of organic nitrogen like blood meal or chicken manure. For most vegetables, as they are going to be growing for a long season, additional side dressings of a liquid nitrogen, such as fish emulsion, may be needed monthly or bimonthly.

While I've stressed nitrogen deficiency, the real trick is to reach a good nitrogen balance in your soil; although plants must have nitrogen to grow, too much causes leaf edges to die, promotes succulent new growth savored by aphids, and makes plants prone to cold damage.

Diseases Caused by Pathogens

Anthracnose is a fungus that is primarily a problem in the eastern United States on beans, tomatoes, cucumbers, and melons. Affected plants develop spots on the leaves; furthermore, beans develop sunken black spots on the pods and stems, and melons, cucumbers, and tomatoes develop sunken spots on the fruits. The disease spreads readily in wet weather and overwinters in the soil on debris. Crop rotation, good air circulation, and choosing resistant varieties are the best defense. Neem-based Green Light Fruit, Nut, and Vegetable Spray gives some control.

Blights and bacterial diseases include a number caused by fungi and bacteria that affect vegetables, and their names hint at the damage they do—blights, wilts, and leaf spots. As a rule, they are more problematic in rainy and humid areas, but given the right conditions, they can be a problem in most of North America. Bacterial wilt affects cucumbers, melons, and sometimes squash. The disease is spread by cucumber beetles and causes the plants to wilt, then die. To diagnose the disease, cut a wilted stem and look for milky sap that forms a thread when the tip of a stick touches it and is drawn away. The disease overwinters in cucumber beetles; cutting their population and installing floating row covers over young plants are the best defenses.

Damping off is caused by a parasitic fungus that lives near the soil surface and attacks young plants in their early seedling stage. It causes them to wilt and fall over just where they emerge from the soil. This fungus thrives under dark, humid conditions, so it can often be thwarted by keeping the seedlings in a bright, well-ventilated place in fast-draining soil. In addition, when possible, start seedlings in sterilized soil.

Fusarium wilt is a soil-borne fungus most prevalent in the warm parts of the country. It causes an overall wilting of the plant visible as the leaves from the base of the plant upward yellow and die. The plants most susceptible to strains of the disease include peppers, cucumber, squash, melons, peas, and basil. While a serious problem in some areas, this disease can be controlled by planting only resistant varieties. Crop rotation is also helpful.

Mildews are fungal diseases that affect some vegetables—particularly peas, spinach, and squash—under certain conditions. There are two types of mildews: powdery and downy. Powdery mildew appears as a white powdery dust on the surface; downy mildew makes velvety or fuzzy white, yellow, or purple patches on leaves, buds, and tender stems. The poorer the air circulation and more humid the weather, the more apt your plants are to have downy mildew.

For both mildews, make sure the plants have plenty of sun and are not crowded by other vegetation. If you must use overhead watering, do it in the morning. In some cases, powdery mildew can be washed off the plant. Do so early in the day, so that the plant has time to dry before evening. Powdery mildew is almost always present at the end of the season on squash and pea

plants but is not a problem because they are usually through producing.

Lightweight summer horticultural oil combined with baking soda has proved effective against powdery mildew on some plants in research at Cornell University. Combine 1 tablespoon of baking soda and 2½ teaspoons of summer oil with 1 gallon of water. Spray weekly. Test on a small part of the plant first. Don't use horticultural oil on very hot days or on plants that are moisture stressed; after applying the oil, wait at least 1 month before using any sulfur sprays on the same plant.

A tea for combating powdery mildew and, possibly, other disease-causing fungi can be made by wrapping 1 gallon of well-aged, manure-based compost in burlap and steeping it in a 5-gallon bucket of water for about 3 days in a warm place. Spray every 3 to 4 days, in the evening if possible, until symptoms disappear.

Root rots and crown rots are caused by a number of fungi. The classic symptom of root rot is wilting—even when a plant is well watered. Sometimes one side of the plant wilts, but more often the whole plant wilts. Affected plants are often stunted and yellow as well. The diagnosis is complete when the dead plant is pulled up to reveal rotten, black roots. Crown rot is a fungus that kills plants at the crown and is primarily

a problem in the Northeast. Root and crown rots are most often caused by poor drainage. There is no cure for root and crown rots once they involve the whole plant. Remove and destroy the plants and correct the drainage problem.

Verticillium wilt is a soil-borne fungus that can be a problem in most of North America, especially the cooler sections. The symptom of this disease is a sudden wilting of one part or all of the plant. If you continually lose tomatoes or eggplants, this, or one of the other wilts, could be the problem. There is no cure, so plant resistant species or varieties if this disease is in your soil.

Viruses attack a number of plants. Symptoms are stunted growth and deformed or mottled leaves. The mosaic viruses destroy chlorophyll in the leaves, causing them to become yellow and blotched in a mosaic pattern. There is no cure for viral conditions, so the affected plants must be destroyed. Cucumbers and beans are particularly susceptible. In the Northwest, pea enation mosaic virus is a problem. Viral diseases can be transmitted by aphids and leaf hoppers, and by seeds, so seed savers should be extra careful to learn the symptoms in individual plant species. When available, use resistant varieties.

resources

The Banana Tree
715 Northampton Street
Easton, PA 18042
No catalog at present; offers seeds of predominantly tropical and subtropical plants, including pigeon peas and ginger, on Web site: www.banana-tree.com

Bamboo Sourcery
666 Wagnon Road
Sebastopol, CA 95472
www.bamboo.nu
The nursery is not open to the public.
$2.00 for catalog; over 200 varieties of bamboo plants

Chiltern Seeds
Bortree Stile
Ulverston
Cumbria LA12 7PB
England
Large variety of different types of seeds

Echo Seed Sales
17430 Durrance Road
North Fort Meyers, FL 33917
$1.00 for catalog
Specializes in tropical and subtropical vegetables and fruits.

Evergreen Y. H. Enterprises
P.O. Box 17538
Anaheim, CA 92817
$2.00 for catalog in USA, $2.50 in Canada; most extensive mail-order selection of Asian vegetables and herbs

Garden City Seeds
778 Highway 93 North
Hamilton, MT 59840
Carries varieties for short seasons and cold climates.

J. L. Hudson, Seedsman
Star Route 2, Box 337
La Honda, CA 94020
For catalog: P.O. Box 1058, Redwood City, CA 94064
$1.00 for catalog; wide selection of seeds, including many hard-to-find varieties

Johnny's Selected Seeds
Foss Hill Road
Albion, ME 04910-9731
Superior varieties of vegetables, herbs, and flowers

Kitazawa Seed Company
1111 Chapman Street
San Jose, CA 95126
Specializes in Asian vegetables

Lilypons Water Gardens
6800 Lilypons Road
P.O. Box 10
Buckeystown, MD 21717
This company specializes in water plants, including water chestnuts

Nichols Garden Nursery
1190 North Pacific Highway NE
Albany, OR 97321-4580
Selected varieties of gourmet vegetables, herbs, and flowers, including several Asian varieties

Redwood City Seed Company
P.O. Box 361
Redwood City, CA 94064
$1.00 for catalog in USA, Canada, Mexico; $2.00 to other countries; specializes in endangered cultivated plants, some Asian.

Richters Herbs
357 Highway 47
Goodwood, Ontario
Canada L0C 1A0
Extensive selection of herb seeds and plants including most of the unusual Southeast Asian ones

Pacific Tree Farms
4301 Lynwood Drive
Chula Vista, CA 91910
$2.00 for catalog; ships live trees and other plants, including Kaffir lime and beecheyana bamboo

Seeds of Change
P.O. Box 15700
Santa Fe, NM 87506-5700
Organically grown vegetable and herb seeds

Seeds Trust High Altitude Gardens
P.O. 1048
Hailey, ID 83333
Specializes in open-pollinated, short-season vegetables and native wildflowers

Shepherd's Garden Seeds
30 Irene Street
Torrington, CT 06790
Excellent varieties of vegetables, herbs, and flowers

Stokes Seeds, Inc.
P.O. Box 548
Buffalo, NY 14240
Vegetable, herb, and flower seeds, including a very good offering of Asian vegetables

Territorial Seed Company
P.O. Box 157
Cottage Grove, OR 97424-0061
Good selection of open-pollinated varieties

Thompson & Morgan, Ltd.
Poplar Lane
Ipswich
Suffolk 1P8 3BU
England
Wide variety of different types of seeds

Tomato Growers Supply Company
P.O. Box 2237
Fort Meyers, FL 33902
Extensive selection of tomatoes and peppers

Upper Bank Nurseries
P.O. Box 486
Media, PA 19063
Carries bamboo plants; send SASE for price list

Van Ness Water Garden
2460 North Euclid Avenue
Upland, CA 91874
Water gardening supplies; carries water chestnut plants; ships in spring and summer only

Vermont Bean Seed Company
Garden Lane
Fair Haven, VT 05743
Extensive selection of beans, including mung and adzuki

Willhite Seed Company Inc.
P.O. Box 23
Poolville, TX 76487
Specializes in warm weather crops, including East Indian vegetables

Gardening and Cooking Supplies

The best source of most Asian ingredients is your local Asian market. If you do not have one near you, Anzen Importers will most likely have what you need.

Anzen Importers
736 Martin Luther King Boulevard
Portland, OR 97232
Many Japanese, Chinese, and Thai dried and canned ingredients

Gardener's Supply Company
128 Intervale Road
Burlington, VT 05401
Gardening tools and supplies

Nutrite, Inc.
P.O. Box 160
Elmira, Ontario
Canada N3B 2Z6
Good Canadian source of gardening supplies

Peaceful Valley Farm Supply
P.O. Box 2209
Grass Valley, CA 95945
Gardening supplies, organic fertilizers, seeds for cover crops

Penzey's Ltd.
P.O. Box 933
Muskego, WI 53150
Large selection of all sorts of dried herbs and spices, including many Asian varieties

Sur la Table
Catalog Division
1765 Sixth Avenue South
Seattle, WA 98134
Cooking equipment

The Oriental Pantry
423 Great Road
Acton, MA 01720
www.orientalpantry.com
Asian groceries and cooking supplies

Williams-Sonoma
Mail Order Department
P.O. Box 7456
San Francisco, CA 94120-7456
Cooking equipment

Annotated Bibliography

Alford, Jeffrey, and Naomi Duguid. *Seductions of Rice: A Cookbook*. New York: Artisan, 1998.
An incredibly good book on rice, filled with history and great recipes.

Andoh, Elizabeth. *At Home with Japanese Cooking*. New York: Knopf, 1980.
This detailed primer on Japanese cooking contains numerous recipes, both simple and complex.

Brennan, Jennifer. *The Original Thai Cookbook*. New York: Berkeley Publishing Group, 1981.
Authentic Thai recipes.

Bubel, Nancy. *The New Seed-Starters Handbook*. Emmaus, Pa.: Rodale Press, 1988.
A must for gardeners interested in starting their own seeds.

Carr, Anna. *Rodale's Color Handbook of Garden Insects*. Emmaus, Pa.: Rodale Press, 1979.
A valuable resource with color photographs to help gardeners identify beneficial and pest insects.

Chan, Peter. *Better Vegetable Gardens the Chinese Way: Peter Chan's Raised-Bed System*. Rev. ed. Pownal, Vt.: Garden Way Publishing, 1985.
This charming book outlines in detail Peter Chan's productive and soil-enriching garden techniques.

Chen, Joyce. *The Joyce Chen Cook Book*. Boston: Joyce Chen Specialty Foods Co., 1983.

Choi, Trieu Thi. *The Food of Vietnam*. Singapore: Periplus, 1997.
Many recipes from Vietnam.

Choudhury, B. *Dr. Vegetables*. New Delhi: National Book Trust, India, 1979.
A compendium of vegetables grown in India, written for growers.

Chu, Lawrence C. C. *Chef Chu's Distinctive Cuisine of China*. New York: Harper & Row, 1983.
This comprehensive book on Chinese cooking contains many photos and recipes.

Cutler, Karan Davis. *Burpee: The Complete Vegetable and Herb Gardener: A Guide to Growing Your Garden Organically*. New York: Macmillan, 1997.
Wonderful, complete guide to organic gardening.

Dahlen, Martha. *A Cook's Guide to Chinese Vegetables*. Hong Kong: Guidebook Company Ltd, 1995.
This little book, with its watercolor illustrations, is invaluable for sorting out Asian vegetables.

Emmons, Didi. *Vegetarian Planet*. Boston: Harvard Common Press, 1997.
A basic vegetarian cookbook with a number of healthy Asian dishes.

Farrelly, David. *The Book of Bamboo*. San Francisco: Sierra Club Books, 1984.
All you could ever want to know about bamboo.

Gilkeson, Linda, Pam Peirce, and Miranda Smith. *Rodale's Pest and Disease Problem Solver: A Chemical-Free Guide to Keeping Your Garden Healthy*. Emmaus, Pa.: Rodale Press, 1996.
Good color photographs of beneficial and pest insects along with lots of sensible advice.

Harrington, Geri. *Grow Your Own Chinese Vegetables*. Pownal, Vt.: Garden Way Publishing, 1984.
Great information on thirty-eight Asian vegetables.

Hom, Ken, and Harvey Steiman. *Chinese Technique: An Illustrated Guide to the Fundamental Techniques of Chinese Cooking*. New York: Simon & Schuster, 1981.
If you want to carve vegetables or make wontons or dozens of other Chinese dishes, here is the place to look for detailed instruction.

Hutton, Wendy. *The Food of India*. Singapore: Periplus Editions, 1998.
Many recipes from India.

———. *The Food of Indonesia*. Singapore: Periplus Editions, 1995.
A selection of recipes from Indonesia.

———. *Tropical Herbs and Spices*. Singapore: Periplus Editions, 1996.
A pocket guide to the basic Asian herbs and spices.

———. *Tropical Vegetables*. Singapore: Periplus Editions, 1996.
A pocket guide to many Asian vegetables.

Jaffrey, Madhur. *A Taste of India*. New York: Atheneum, 1986.
This fabulous book covers both the cooking and the culture of India.

Konishi, Kiyoko. *Japanese Cooking for Health and Fitness*. Tokyo: Gakken Company Ltd., 1983.
A valuable primer on Japanese cooking; includes many recipes for vegetables.

Kushi, Aveline. *Complete Guide to Macrobiotic Cooking*. New York: Warner Books, 1985.
A primer for vegetarian cooking using on many Japanese foods.

Larkcom, Joy. *Oriental Vegetables: The Complete Guide for Garden and Kitchen*. Tokyo: Kodansha International, 1991.
The definitive book on growing Asian vegetables, a must-have.

Liley, Vicki. *Wok*. Singapore: Periplus Editions, 1998.
Lots of ideas for cooking stir-fries.

Nix, Janeth Johnson. *Adventures in Oriental Cooking*. San Francisco: Ortho Books, 1976.
Here's a fine how-to book for beginners and experienced cooks alike on using Asian vegetables.

Olkowski, William, Sheila Daar, and Helga Olkowski. *The Gardener's Guide to Common-Sense Pest Control*. Newtown, Conn.: Taunton Press, 1995.
Thoroughly researched information on pest control for the home gardener.

Passmore, Jacki. *Asia: The Beautiful Cookbook*. Los Angeles: Knapp Press, 1987.
Lots of recipes and cultural information.

———. *The Complete Chinese Cookbook*. Boston: Charles E. Tuttle Company, 1998.
A great overview of Chinese cooking with lots of history and recipes.

Rau, Santha Rama. *The Cooking of India*. New York: Time-Life, 1969.
A basic cultural overview and recipes from many parts of India.

Saville, Carole. *Exotic Herbs*. New York: Henry Holt and Company, 1997.
Superb growing and culinary advice on many herbs, including most Asian ones, spiced with fascinating herb history from one of today's most knowledgeable herb mavens.

Shimizu, Shinko. *New Salads: Quick Healthy Recipes from Japan*. Tokyo: Kodansha International Ltd., 1986.

Many healthy and interesting salad ideas.

Solomon, Charmaine. *Charmaine Solomon's Encyclopedia of Asian Foods.* Boston: Periplus Editions Ltd., 1996.
A must-have for Asian cooking.

———. *The Complete Asian Cookbook.* Rutland, Vt: Charles E. Tuttle Company, 1995.
A helpful compendium of Asian recipes.

Takahashi, Kuwako. *The Joy of Japanese Cooking.* Tokyo: Shufunotomo Co., Ltd., 1986.
Lots of basic information on ingredients and Japanese specialties.

Tindall, H. D. *Vegetables in the Tropics.* London: MacMillan Press Ltd., 1983.
How to grow many vegetables under warm conditions.

spices, including many Asian varieties

Tropp, Barbara. *The Modern Art of Chinese Cooking.* New York: Morrow, 1982.
This book, a compendium of information on Chinese food, is most valuable for Western cooks. Numerous reliable recipes, both authentic and adapted to Western ingredients.

Tsuji, Shizuo. *Practical Japanese Cooking.* Tokyo: Kodansha International, 1986.
Many basic Japanese recipes.

Van, Paulette Do. *Vietnamese Cooking.* Secaucus, N. J.: Chartwell Books, 1993.
A good overall look at Vietnamese cooking, though short on vegetables and herbs.

Yamagushi, Eri. *The Well-Flavored Vegetable.* Tokyo: Kodansha International, 1988.
Traditional and new vegetable recipes from Japan.

Other Resources

American Horticulture Society. "The Heat Map." 1-800-777-7931, Extension 45. Cost: $15.00.

acknowledgments

My garden is the foundation for my books, photography, and recipes. For nearly twelve months of the year we toil to keep it beautiful and bountiful. Unlike most gardens, as it is a photo studio and trial plot, it must look glorious, be healthy, and produce for the kitchen all year. To complicate the maintenance, all the beds are changed every spring and fall. Needless to say, this is a large undertaking. For two decades, a quartet of talented organic gardener-cooks have not only given it hundreds of hours of loving attention but also been generous with their vast knowledge of plants. Together we have forged our concept of gardening and cooking, much of which I share with you in this series of garden cookbooks.

I wish to thank Wendy Krupnick for giving the garden such a strong foundation and Joe Queirolo for maintaining it so beautifully for many years. For the last decade, Jody Main and Duncan Minalga have helped me expand my garden horizons. No matter how complex the project, they enthusiastically rise to the occasion. In the kitchen, I am most fortunate to have Gudi Ritter, a talented cook who sees all new recipes as a welcome challenge. I thank her for the help she provides as we create recipes and present them in all their glory.

I thank Dayna Lane for her steady hand and editorial assistance. In addition to day-to-day compilations, she joins me on our constant search for the most effective organic pest controls, superior vegetable varieties, and the best sources for plants.

Gardeners are by nature most generous. I want to thank Carole Saville, who guides me through the maze of Asian herbs and gives trusted input on recipes. Many seeds people help me amass variety and growing information from all over the county. I particularly want to thank Renee Shepherd of Shepherd's Garden Seeds and Rose Marie Nichols McGee of Nichols Garden Nursery.

Over the last three decades, my Asian education has been greatly aided by many friends, neighbors, and professionals. I fortunately live in a part of the world richly populated with people either native to Asia or who are Asian scholars. For years, my daily walks were filled with stories of India and neighbors answering questions like, "What's available in Taiwan?" and "Does your mother make this in Vietnam?" And Asian cookbooks and equipment are willingly loaned. Further, I get to tag along with these patient folks to every sort of Asian grocery store, with guides who not only grew up with most of the vegetables in question but can translate food labels and ask detailed questions of the clerks. My neighbor Cheryl Chang sends seeds from Asia and reports on what's in the markets. In particular, I am most grateful to Arvind and Bhadra Fancy, Helen and Ramsay Chang, and Henry Tran and Mai Truong. Many of their favorite recipes are included in the book. Ellen Brandon, an Asian scholar and devotee of Japanese cooking, has been most generous with information and has shared her library.

Interviews with gardener Peter Chan and chef Ken Hom were of great value, as were conversations and a tour of Chinese markets with chef Barbara Tropp. Being able to share garden experiences with David Cunningham in his Vermont garden gave me confidence that Asian vegetables are oh so adaptable. These people's vast view of Asian vegetables enriches the information throughout the book.

I would also like to thank my husband, Robert, who gives such high-quality technical advice and loving support.

Many people were instrumental in bringing this book project to fruition. They include Jane Whitfield, Linda Gunnarson, and David Humphrey, who were integral to the initial vision of this book; Kathryn Sky-Peck, who provided the style and quality of the layout, and Marcy Hawthorne, who made the lovely drawings. Heartfelt thanks to Eric Oey and to the entire Periplus staff, especially Deane Norton and Jan Johnson, for their help. Finally, I would like to thank my editor, Jeanine Caunt, for her strong presence, many talents, and dedication to quality.